Second Cup
of Coffee

Second Cup of Coffee

Proverbs for Today's Woman

Jean Shaw

ZONDERVAN
PUBLISHING HOUSE
OF THE ZONDERVAN CORPORATION
GRAND RAPIDS, MICHIGAN 49506

Second Cup of Coffee
Copyright © 1981 by The Zondervan Corporation

Scripture quotations, unless otherwise indicated, are from
The Holy Bible: The New International Version, copyright
© 1978 by the New York International Bible Society. Used
by permission.

Designed by Art Jacobs
Illustrated by Martha Bentley

Library of Congress Cataloging in Publication Data

Shaw, Jean.
    Second cup of coffee.

    1. Women—Prayer-books and devotions—English. 2.
Bible. O.T. Proverbs—Meditations. I. Title.
BV4844.S53   242'.643   80-39577
ISBN 0-310-43542-0

Printed in the United States of America

82 83 84 85 86 87 88 — 10 9 8 7 6 5

To Mary Anne

"Perfume and incense bring joy to the heart, and the pleasantness of one's friend springs from her earnest counsel."

—*Proverbs 27:9*

Second Cup of Coffee

PREFACE

Over half the women in the United States are employed outside the home. This fact comes as no surprise to you. Either you're one of the employed, or you're frustrated because you can't find enough women at home to teach VBS this summer. If recruiting isn't your responsibility, just spend one morning doing door-to-door visitation. You won't find many people answering doorbells.

Another interesting statistic is that half the marriages in the United States have ended in divorce. The divorce rate is slowly increasing, and so is the marriage rate. That means being married is still a popular option, even for those whose first relationship didn't last.

For a rapidly growing number of people, living together without being married is a comfortable arrangement. It may not be comfortable for their parents, but it is nevertheless practiced with very little personal guilt or public censure.

On the other hand, it's now O.K. to be single and state that you like being your own person. You can go to church without fear of some deacon's wife inviting you home to dinner, just so you can meet that "nice twenty-eight-year-old boy who works in the hobby shop."

Two things are sure. First, there is no "average woman." You can't generalize about homemakers or nurses or even doctors anymore. And second, women who stay home all day and care for their families are either old, on TV reruns, or very unusual people.

We ought to scrap all the beauty pageants and have one for Ms. America. She's the real United States woman. This book is written for her.

"Listen, my son,
to your father's instruction,
and do not forsake
your mother's teaching."

(Prov. 1:8)

My mother told me I'd be sorry that I didn't practice my piano lessons, and she was right. Whenever I'm asked to play the piano at an evening service, I hope someone will request "Trust and Obey," instead of "Wonderful Grace of Jesus."

My mother still tells me things: "Don't work so hard"; "Put your feet up"; "That button is dangling. Get me a needle and thread." Every time she comes for a visit, she whips me into shape.

It has been said that to a mother a son is always twelve years old. Even when a middle-aged meteorologist is in his parental home his mother will hand him his overcoat as he leaves the house, in case the weather turns cold. When I go home, my mother makes sure I have two quarters to pay the bus driver.

Parenting never stops. While we're pouring out advice to our children, our parents are pouring in advice to us. If they didn't, we'd soon be empty and dried up from lack of concern. Sure, we protest being told what to do: "I'm fifty years old, Mom. I think I know when it's time to go to bed!" But it's still a good feeling to be the object of someone's love.

"Honor your father and your mother" doesn't have a time limit. God's commandment applies to the nursing infant and continues to the nursing home. I'm resenting parental instruction less and less as I realize how much of what they tried to teach me made good sense.

I'm not too old to learn from my father and mother, Lord. Make me appreciative of their instruction. Give me respect for their wisdom.

Call your mother or father on the phone today and let one of them give you some good advice. 🍵

"Do not be wise
in your own eyes;
fear the Lord
and shun evil.
This will bring health
to your body,
and nourishment
to your bones."

(Prov. 3:7–8)

The idea that goodness is related to good health is backed up by solid medical proof. According to one medical study in Israel several years ago, synagogue-attending Sabbath observers were found to have significantly fewer coronaries than non-observers. Resting one day in seven is not God's arbitrariness, but His love.

The anxiety and tensions that result from lack of trust in the Lord make our backs and heads ache, our stomachs upset, our intestines malfunction, and our hearts break down. Overindulgence in food and drink affects every part of the body, making us fat and creating other health problems. The results of promiscuity are also provable. Venereal disease is not a problem with married couples who limit their sexual activities to each other.

Since a woman's body is a temple of the Holy Spirit, she must take good care of it. The Bible has a surprising amount of practical advice on work, recreation, diet, and even sleeping. Try Psalm 4 when you're lying awake at two in the morning.

God knows we all like to think we know what is best for ourselves. The friend who suggests we take a vacation or says, "Why don't you see a doctor?" isn't always appreciated. We don't realize we're snapping at the children, or neglecting our appearance. We think we're our usual good-natured, capable selves.

Proper awe of the Lord and His Word, followed by obedience, will actually improve our health. This proper relationship with the Lord will nourish our bones, keeping them resistant to breakage and the curvature that comes with old age. The relationship of diet and exercise to bone content isn't as far-fetched as we once thought. When we need to shun evil, a healthy spirit in a healthy body makes it much easier.

Lord, I confess that I have not been obedient. I have not always avoided evil, and my soul and body are suffering. Help me to discipline my life. Give me better health as I bring it into conformity with your Word.

If you had to throw off every weight that besets you, how long would it take you before you could run? ☕

"Honor the Lord
with your wealth,
with the firstfruits
of all your crops;
then your barns will be
filled to overflowing,
and your vats will
brim with new wine."

(Prov. 3:9–10)

This is not a choice, but a commandment. All that we own is to be used to bring credit to God's name. Friday's paycheck already belongs to Him. When we use it to buy groceries, pay taxes, or get the car fixed, we have to evaluate our spending from the point of view of good management. This leads to such complications as driving five miles to pick up a special on cheddar cheese. Does the cost of gasoline exceed the savings on the cheese?

The Israelite farmer had an easier task. When his crops ripened, he took the first harvest and gave it to the priests. This doesn't mean we need to collect all our cucumbers and zucchini and give them to the minister. I knew a minister's wife who said that in August she hated to open the door to the back porch because she knew it would be piled high with hubbard squash, green beans, and tomatoes. As quickly as she got them all processed, another batch would appear, left by loving church members who thought she really enjoyed canning.

First fruits, in this instance, can be considered ten percent—the Biblical tithe. God is given His portion first, before the rent is paid. We spend what is left. This principle runs counter to the usual practice of paying all our bills and then giving God any coins we've got lying around.

With the commandment comes the promise that God will supply all our needs and more, to the point of overflowing. God may rearrange our priorities, and take away certain desires, but the promise holds true. As we honor the Lord with our wealth, so He will bless us.

I have so many bills, Lord. I'm always needing something, and with this inflation, it's getting harder to manage my money. Help me to give you the firstfruits, and seek your guidance as to how I should spend the rest.

Once we're in a store, we always buy more than we planned to. See how many days you can go without shopping for anything. ☕

> "Do not withhold good
> from those who deserve it,
> when it is in
> your power to act.
> Do not say to your neighbor,
> 'Come back later.
> I'll give it tomorrow'—
> when you now have it with you."
>
> (Prov. 3:27–28)

It has been said that good intentions are like ghosts hovering about in need of bodies. I've had my share of the wispy things—making a hospital visit two days after the patient goes home; promising to take a friend out to lunch and never getting around to it; planning to share

16

the gospel with a neighbor and discovering that she's divorced and moved away.

While not doing a helpful deed when we've thought of it is very sad, how much worse is our refusal to help a neighbor when we're able. If she'd only ask when we weren't so busy, like between nine and ten Tuesday mornings. But no, the request comes through just as we're off to our Bible study, or putting together a spaghetti casserole. Absolutely the worst time is during our favorite TV show. Just as Lou Grant steps into the elevator to get the big story, our telephone rings.

Scripture stipulates that we are to do good when it is in our power. If our neighbor needs to borrow an egg, and we have one egg, we are to give it to her. Tomorrow's breakfast will be cereal instead of pancakes. If she needs our time, and we have time (if we are not going to the hospital for an operation or catching a plane) we are to give her that. Tomorrow we will do what we couldn't do today and not be anxious about it.

Next year we may not have an extra egg or extra time, and then the opportunity to help will be lost. God may choose to take our abundance away from us, or take us away from our abundance. Later we may be asking a neighbor for an egg or an hour's time.

Thank you, God, for all those who have shared good with me. Thank you for those special friends and neighbors who give without question or hesitation. Help me to do the same.

Do you know your neighbors well enough to understand what their needs really are? 🍵

"Drink water from your own cistern, running water from your own well."

(Prov. 5:15)

I was getting dressed in the locker room of a racquet club when two young women came in. As if I weren't there at all, they carried on a lively discussion about what they were going to get their boyfriends for Christmas. A pendant on a gold chain was first choice. They went on from there to talk about what they would buy their husbands. Clothes, probably. Maybe a sweater.

For some people, the problem with adultery is nothing more than a dilemma of Christmas shopping. Morality has long since become passé. Even the ethical relationships approach is out of date. Sexual passion is to be satisfied, whether it's a one-night stand in a resort motel room, or "working late" twice a week.

God says when we're thirsty we are to get a drink of water at home. He is simple and direct. No allowance for the frustrated traveling salesman, or the person married to a partner who only knows two positions and wears pajamas in bed. Whatever the problems, a husband and wife are to confine their sexual activity to each other. No matter how a person rationalizes, adultery is flatly condemned.

Of course, God has His reasons. He knows that we are blessed by the persons and relationships in a true family. From the family comes our security, and in the family we realize our potential. It is also the family that gives us a sense of continuity—a belonging to the past, present, and future.

"Let them [sexual passions] be yours alone, never to be shared with strangers," says Proverbs 17. Obedience will bring joy and true love. "Fooling around" is never really secret. Someone finds out. God has a full view of it, because "he examines all our paths." Our evil deeds will eventually ensnare us, binding us like cords so that there is no escape. Our lack of discipline will lead to a tormented death.

Everybody's doing it, Lord, and it's hard to be faithful. Temptations are everywhere. Even if my body is faithful, my mind is full of lust. Help me to curb my desires. Make me content to have sex with my husband, and with no one else.

For further study on sexual relations: 1 Corinthians 7. ☕

"For a wise son brings
joy to his father,
but a foolish son
grief to his mother."

(Prov. 10:1)

The Bible has much to say to the foolish son. But what about the grieving mother? Where is her comfort as she watches him obsessed with drugs, or irresponsibly shifting from one job to another? He makes a bad marriage and returns to lick his wounds under the family roof. Late one night she gets a telephone call from the state police. John Jr. was picked up for speeding. He was clocked at eighty-two miles an hour, and there were thirteen empty beer cans in the back seat!

It is easy to point a finger and say, "Mother, you failed. It's all your fault. With guilt added to grief, life takes on a perpetual heaviness, a sense of despair. How did this happen? I tried to be a good mother. I didn't neglect my son. I went to all the school activities, the sports events, the church programs. My other children turned out well. Why is he like this?

There is no slick answer. Even prolonged analysis may be inconclusive. We cannot fathom the intricasies of a person's mind. Research in child behavior indicates chemical imbalance and diet as possibilities. Only God knows the heart.

In this there is comfort. God knows our hearts too. He recognizes our good intentions. Where we have sinned, we can seek His forgiveness, receive it, and be at peace. Christ has borne our guilt on the cross, and paid the price for it. Alleluia!

The Bible offers further counsel. There is a time of accountability in each person's life, when he can no longer blame anyone else for what he does. Whatever our past, we can, through faith in Jesus Christ, become new creatures. The renegade child can use guilt as a means to keep his parents in bondage. "You are to blame for my sins," he says in effect. "Now you must do whatever I ask, to make up for it." To this we can say, "No!", and claim the power to free ourselves. The relocation of responsibility may be the very act God uses to bring the foolish son to repentance and faith.

Oh, God, I cannot live my children's lives. Indwell them with your Holy Spirit and guide them through your teaching. Free me to serve you as the person I am today. Thank you.

For further insight, read Ezekiel 18 and Romans 9.

"He who gathers crops
in summer is a wise son,
but he who sleeps during harvest
is a disgraceful son."

(Prov. 10:5)

It is estimated that at least 70 percent of the homes in our country will grow at least one vegetable plant this year. From patio tomatoes to ten feet by twenty-six feet plots, America is into gardening.

A person would have to be foolish indeed to grow vegetables and never pick them. Even if she can't use all the green beans herself, she should pick them and give them away for the sake of the plants. Regular picking encourages new production.

Another thing a gardener discovers is that late August and early September is the time when yields are heaviest. Canning or freezing must be done then. Squash won't stop growing while the gardener is on vacation. The zucchini will keep right on expanding, going from slender, tender cylinders to monstrous tough footballs with bitter flavor.

This proverb commends diligence. Note something else. The one who works hard is a wise *son*. Why a son, and not simply a man? Because our degree of effort affects other people. We may not care about prospering, but we have others in the family to consider. Our laziness affects their good name and their reputation. It also makes us a burden to them. When we neglect our gardens, they have to come over to weed. If the crop is a complete failure, they feel obligated to give us their carrots and green peppers. They don't mind sharing, but they'd like to get a cabbage or two in return.

Help me, Lord, to keep my part of the family garden in good condition. Make me a consistent worker from spring tilling to autumn harvest.

Example of a diligent son who knew how to garden: Genesis 41:46–57. ☕

> "The wise in heart
> accepts commands,
> but a chattering fool
> comes to ruin."
>
> (Prov. 10:8)

I used to engage in long religious discussions with a man who could not understand how all the people in the world came from Adam and Eve. No matter where we started our thinking—the birth of Jesus, Paul's journeys, even Samson, we ended up with the same question about populating the earth. I despaired of any spiritual breakthrough. Indeed, I wondered why the population of the earth was more significant to him than the basic issues of salvation and the Christian life.

Years later the man was graciously saved, and I was

amazed at how his favorite topic no longer mattered. It was then that I realized his constant returning to Adam and Eve was "chattering"—a diversive talking of minor matters to avoid the real issue of the state of his soul.

Chattering fools turn up in Bible classes and discussion groups all the time. Rather than listen, they ask many questions and engage in long discussions which drive the other members of the group into a frustrated frenzy. These are the same people who wander from church to church, staying long enough in each one to exhaust the patience of all those who are the targets of their interminable debating.

It is not the spirit of inquiry that is objectionable. Anyone who loves the Scriptures is happy to answer questions about them. But the chattering fool will not listen to the answers.

A teachable spirit is evidence of a sincere faith. When Christ is our Lord and Savior, His Holy Spirit lives in us and prepares our hearts to learn God's law and to do it. Paul says, "We have not received the spirit of the world but the Spirit who is from God, that we may understand what God has freely given us ... the man without the Spirit does not accept the things that come from the Spirit of God, for they are foolishness to him, and he cannot understand them, because they are spiritually discerned" (1 Cor. 2:12, 14).

Is there a command from Scripture that you have refused to obey? Perhaps you are wise in heart but in need of more teaching. Or perhaps your heart really does not belong to Christ, and your chattering disguises your true spiritual condition. Since the ruin or salvation of your soul is at stake, it is crucial that you know the difference.

Dear God, give me a teachable spirit.

A test to see if you are a fool: Proverbs 1:7. ☕

> "He who conceals his hatred
> has lying lips, and
> whoever spreads slander
> is a fool."
>
> (Prov. 10:18)

After years of wrestling with the problem of honesty versus tact, our family settled upon the word "interesting." If the soloist is terrible, but you have to say something to her, you comment that her choice of songs was most "interesting." When the dinner includes a strange piece of meat that resembles boiled door mat, the guest tells the cook that the meal was certainly "interesting." "Interesting" also covers those situations in which you have to respond to kindergarten art work, seventh grade sewing projects, and your son's first apartment.

Such commentary is accepted social practice. As an alternative to ego-smashing criticism it is preferable. It does contain an element of truth, and you have left the way open for a deeper evaluation once a caring relationship is established.

This is good, but not good enough. Jesus calls His followers to love one another in such a way that all men will know we belong to Him (John 13:34–35). As we eat the tough meat we must love the hostess and find in her something truly praiseworthy. (She is hospitable. And the salad was delicious.) The off-key soloist—perhaps she doesn't feel well, her accompanist was new, a family problem is bothering her. And it was kind of her to take the trouble to attend the meeting. Son, your taste in decoration isn't mine, but I admire your independence and appreciate being invited over. (Many parents aren't even asked.)

"Rid yourselves of all malice, all deceit, hypocrisy, envy and slander of every kind," says 1 Peter 2:1. How can we do that? "You have tasted that the Lord is good" (v. 3). Into the heart the Holy Spirit pours love. This flows out again through the mouth in the form of refreshing, sweet words free of hatred, lying, and slander.

Oh Father, there are some people I find impossible to love. There are times when I cannot think of a kind thing to say. Refresh me with your Spirit, that I may refresh others.

Another look at words and water: John 4:1–26. ☕

"When words are many,
sin is not absent,
but he who holds
his tongue is wise."

(Prov. 10:19)

It must be wonderful to speak in public!" exclaims the quiet person to me after a banquet. Wonderful sometimes, yes, but terribly dangerous. A captive audience, opportunity to influence them, ego of being "star on stage," and nervousness all cause the mouth to say peculiar things. "Do you write out your speeches?" Oh yes! Without a script I would ramble all over the place and say something that wasn't true, or hurt somebody's feelings.

I wonder if quiet people ever appreciate their blessings. How wonderful it must be to say nothing. Verbal people always have a profound comment, an earth-shaking statement they have to get out. They sit on the edge of their chairs, interrupting the interruptions, while the non-verbal souls wait patiently for a chance to add something really important.

Harder still is saying nothing when we're attacked. The sharp answer rises into the larynx, pushing to explode through the lips. Satan urges us to "let him have it," "Tell her off," "Put her in her place." Once the words start they keep coming, leading us deeper and deeper into sin.

There is help. James charges us to submit ourselves to God. We must humble ourselves and draw near to Him. There is hope. Jesus died for our sins of the tongue. He is ready to forgive us, when we are truly sorry.

"Set a guard over my mouth, O Lord; keep watch over the door of my lips" (Ps. 141:3).

Read James 4 today.

"A good listener is not only popular everywhere, but after a while he gets to know something" (Wilson Mizner).

> "As vinegar to the teeth
> and smoke to the eyes,
> so is a sluggard to those
> who send him."

(Prov. 10:26)

Father was away when the boys decided to use the fireplace. They piled in wood and newspaper, set them afire and watched the flames shoot up. The smoke, however, did not shoot up. It shot out into the room, and in seconds filled the house. No one had thought to open the damper! We ran next door and got our neighbor, who came running with a metal pole. He jammed it against the damper, gave a hard push, and the flue opened, allowing the roaring blaze to send its smoke up the chimney. Crying and gasping for breath, we opened all the windows. It was an hour before our eyes cleared. It was two days before I stopped smelling like I had been camping.

It doesn't take a smoking fireplace to irritate the eyes. One cigarette in the doctor's waiting room can bring tears. With the smarting eyes comes a rising irritation at the smoker, who puffs away, completely unaware of anyone else in the room.

Like fireplace smoke which burns the eyes, and a smoker who doesn't realize she's bothering anyone, so is the sluggard. What is curious about this proverb is that it doesn't say he's a problem to those to whom he's sent, although that is certainly true. We are told that this sluggard aggravates the people who send him. Who could they be?

They could be the church, suffering a bad reputation from its members who claim to know and love Christ, but show little evidence of it in their lives. They worship on Sunday, pay their pledge, even have daily devotions, but they're half asleep while doing it, lacking zeal and passion. Week after week they hear the sermon challenging them to work while it is still day. Through glazed eyes they look at others in the congregation and think the message is surely for them. After the benediction, they shuffle out, no more repentant or enthusiastic than when they came in.

What about the vinegar? It sets the teeth on edge, burns the throat, and brings tears to the eyes. Maybe that's the way ministers feel about the sluggards in their church.

Father, I am sure that I irritate someone with my carelessness, without having any idea that I'm doing it. Show me where I'm vinegar and smoke. Make me alive and eager to serve you.

Can a person be a faithful church worker and still be a sluggard? See Romans 12. ☕

"Wealth is worthless
in the day of wrath,
but righteousness delivers
from death."

(Prov. 11:4)

In Revelation 6:15–17, we read of a great day of wrath, when everyone, rich and poor, slave and free, will stand before the Lamb of God for His judgment. Those who have sincerely professed their salvation in Jesus Christ will worship Him in heaven forever. Those who have rejected

Him will spend their eternity in hell. One's status in society, or personal fortune, will make no difference at all. God will look upon the heart to see if it has been cleansed from sin by the blood of the Lamb.

It is significant that the Holy Spirit directed the writers of Scripture to use the word "wrath" to describe God's attitude toward those who will not acknowledge His Son. "Wrath" is an old English word coming from "wroth," which means predictable anger. We know ahead of time what God will do. It is no surprise, no capricious decision based upon His whim and feeling at the moment. The warning is clear.

We can be just as sure of God's decision if we have righteousness—the quality of being right with God through the atoning work of Christ. "God made him (Jesus) who had no sin to be sin for us, so that in him we might become the righteousness of God" (2 Cor. 5:21). It's no surprise, no capricious decision. Eternal life is sure.

God wants us to know where we stand with Him, and He does not make that standing dependent upon our personal fortune. If we are not righteous, He invites us to become so. He desires that we all be delivered from death, "not wanting anyone to perish, but everyone to come to repentance" (2 Peter 3:9).

O Lamb of God, salvation and glory and power belong to you. True and just are your judgments. I thank you for dying on the cross for me. I thank you that I have eternal life with you. I thank you that I can be sure of this.

How will the surety that you are going to heaven affect the work that you do today? 🍵

> "A kind-hearted woman
> gains respect,
> but ruthless men
> gain only wealth."
>
> (Prov. 11:16)

When my mother wants to describe an especially kind person, she says she has a "heart of gold."

A heart of gold, of course, is worth much more than its material value. It is the essence of a person who is sensitive to the needs of others and responds appropriately. Some of us never see where other people are hurting. Some see, but do nothing. Others see, and do the wrong thing. There is a well-known story about a young woman who was concerned for her fiancé who walked to work every day, even in the coldest weather. She knit him a red, wool scarf, only to discover that he didn't like red, was allergic to wool, and never wore scarves. At least she attempted to be kind.

Early in the history of the Jews, they were commanded to be kind to strangers (Lev. 19:34). God also expects us to be kind to our neighbors, the poor, orphans, widows, and those in prison. Jesus even tells us to love our enemies (Luke 6:34). Paul and Peter put special emphasis upon kindness to others in our church.

Do we find it curious that the Scriptures do not make more mention of kindness in the family? A possible reason may be that God expects us to treat our partners and our children as respectfully as we do others. Therefore, all Scripture concerning forgiveness, compassion, longsuffering, courtesy, and the like applies to them just as it applies to those in the church and in our neighborhoods. To our shame, our kindness is often much greater outside the home than in it. Thus we see the mother who patiently ministers to every sick family in the block, but is short-tempered to her own children and the wife who encourages a depressed neighbor, but criticizes her husband in front of their friends.

"Charity begins at home" is a much-abused saying. But when considered as the starting point for kindness to extend to the whole world, it aligns our priorities properly. After all, if a woman is not respected by her own family, it matters little how much she is respected anywhere else.

Lord, I am often least kind to those closest to me. I assume they'll put up with me, no matter how thoughtless I am. Forgive me. Show me ways to express my love for my family. Help me to make them feel special.

Think of one special act of kindness you can perform for each member of your family today. Sew on a button. Put a note of encouragement in a lunch box. Hug hard. Make sure you do these things. ☕

> "Like a gold ring
> in a pig's snout
> is a beautiful woman
> who shows no discretion."

(Prov. 11:22)

We have a culturally determined standard for beauty, which some people meet, and some don't. Fortunately, relationships are determined for other reasons, so those of us not noted for our faces and figures need not feel sorry for ourselves. We find exceeding comfort in the truism that love is blind. We can be thankful for that.

It isn't wrong to be beautiful. A woman noted for being attractive doesn't need to apologize. God made her that way, and nothing God does is useless. But beauty has power, and when an impure character is clothed in physical loveliness, what appears to be an angel is Satan in disguise, looking for someone to devour.

Discretion is the quality of making good judgments in speech and behavior. The resource for saying and doing the right thing is the Bible, not magazines, talk-shows, hair stylists, or even friends, unless they accept God's Word as true. The beautiful woman must be especially careful where she gets her counsel, since she has the potential for greater influence. A beautiful high-school teacher can lead or mislead hundreds of teen-age girls who admire her for typifying their TV-oriented image of the ideal woman. She can encourage them to be God's saints or Charlie's angels.

A beautiful woman without descretion is dangerous around men. She can manipulate them to her advantage, in the board room and the bedroom. Such deception takes its toll, of course, and she finds no true joy. A pig with a gold ring in his snout is still a pig.

I'm not a fashion model, Lord, but I'd like to be a model of Christlikeness. I'd like to have true beauty, and be helpful and kind, loving and encouraging. Draw me deep into your Word for the discretion I need. And please, God, make me a beautiful woman in the eyes of someone else.

If beauty is not condemned, how much time and money should we spend to look as attractive as possible? ☕

"The fruit of the righteous
is a tree of life; and
he who wins souls
is wise."

(Prov. 11:30)

Soul-winning is honorable and difficult work. It requires involvement in a person's life. Once we step across the threshold into her soul, we enter a territory which will require some adjustment in our own life-style. We find ourselves doing strange things, like going bowling when we can hardly lift up the ball, and drinking coffee with cream and sugar when we really like tea with lemon. Our carefully planned presentation of the gospel falls apart as the potential convert asks, "How could Adam and Eve ever have grandchildren?"

Soul-winning takes wisdom. We must search the Scriptures for the passages that will be most helpful. We must know when to press on, and when to wait. The whole question of accommodation drives us to prayer. If a friend invites us to a Sunday barbeque, should we go? We don't usually go to parties on Sunday, and there will be a lot of beer drinking, and ... but this is her way of expressing love. To refuse would make us appear unfriendly and make our Christianity into a religion of "you can't do that's."

As the relationship intensifies, our souls lose a layer of clothing, too. Our witness comes under scrutiny. Are we really trustworthy? Do we really care about the other women at work? When Mr. Hubble tells his dirty stories, do we have to keep from laughing?

God promises that our righteousness will bear fruit. Indeed, we shall see our seeds of the gospel sprout into trees of people who accept Jesus Christ as their Lord and Savior. Trees, of course, take time to germinate. Apple seeds are planted in the fall, kept at a temperature of forty degrees over the winter, and expected to sprout the following spring. Once an apple seed sprouts, it requires constant attention if it is going to become a disease-resistant, fruit-bearing tree itself.

Frankly, Lord, when it comes to soul-winning, I don't want to get involved in someone's life. I don't want someone else involved in mine. I don't believe that people without Christ are really lost. Give me this realization, Lord. Give me the concern and wisdom I need to be an effective witness. And then Lord, give me mature fruit.

This week, ask someone you don't know very well to have lunch with you. As you talk, be alert for mention of some hobby or interest which will give you reason to develop a friendship. ☕

"A wife of noble character
is her husband's crown,
but a disgraceful wife
is like decay in his bones."

(Prov. 12:4)

A crown is a symbol of distinction. You have to be somebody important to wear one. If I started wearing a crown to the supermarket, the other customers would wonder if I had just won a jogging race, or been declared the best hamburger cook in the neighborhood. I can't wear a crown just because I feel like it.

Noble character indicates quality and strength. A wife with those qualities gives her husband distinction. He is somebody important. Oh, when you see him working on the assembly line, you may not think so;/but he knows he is special, and his wife knows he is special, and their marriage is a little more extraordinary than other people's.

A disgraceful wife, on the other hand, rather than build her husband up, tears him down. Not all at once, but little by little, she corrodes him. Over the years her infidelity, or bad temper, or jealousy eats away at his self-esteem, making him feel like a worthless failure. So he doesn't do well at work, being tired and preoccupied. Eventually his personality shrivels up.

Some wives today believe it's wrong for a husband to be a king. Yes it is, if the wife is a slave. But the Bible never teaches a wife to be a slave. She is to have noble character, embodying quality and strength. She is royalty too, a co-partner of a king. She becomes a queen, the most important woman in the kingdom.

Have I ever been a disgraceful wife, Lord? Maybe I've torn my husband down in little ways. Forgive me. Encourage and strengthen me through the power of your Holy Spirit so that I can be a source of encouragement. and strength to him.

Write down five things that you can do this week to make your husband feel like a king. ☕

"An anxious heart
weighs a man down,
but a kind word
cheers him up."

(Prov. 12:25)

Ellen had changed her dress three times. Then she decided she was wearing the wrong shoes. She recombed her hair, taking out the little fuzzies over her ears that the hair dresser had said were so chic. "It's not me," Ellen decided, giving a last look in the mirror. She checked her purse again to be sure she had her glasses, a comb, and a good pen. She read the map for the tenth time. It was supposed to be a ten-minute drive, but she was leaving a half hour early, just in case.

What if they didn't like her? What if she made a mistake —tripped over the rug or got stuck in the elevator? Her stomach was getting queasy. She could still taste her morning poached egg on toast. The jangle of the phone was a decided annoyance, just as she was going out the door.

It was Kaye. "I know your first day on the new job is going to be great. You're perfectly suited for it, you know. Everything you've been doing these past fifteen years has prepared you for this experience. Think of all the organizational work you've done at the church. You'll fit in without any trouble. I'll be praying with you all through the day."

Suddenly Ellen saw the day as a bright challenge. Kaye was right. She had learned a lot since she got out of college: managing a home, running VBS, organizing the women's society at church. She wasn't exactly a neophyte in administration. And she wasn't over the hill physically, by any means. She was certainly still able to work hard.

Kaye's phone call had made all the difference. How kind of her to call! She knew Kaye was praying with her. Ellen remembered how often they had studied Philippians 4:6—"Do not be anxious about anything, but in everything, by prayer and petition, with thanksgiving, present your requests to God."

She stopped in the front hall and asked God again to guide her through the day. Then she gave a final look in the mirror. She didn't need those fuzzies one bit. With a light heart she hurried to the car.

Thank you, Lord, for all those people who have reassured me when I was feeling anxious. Make me sensitive to other people's needs. Use me to cheer up those who are discouraged, to praise those who need encouragement. May I be a heart lightener.

Send a greeting card to someone who needs a lift in spirits right now. ☕

"The wise woman
builds her house,
but with her own hands
the foolish one
tears hers down."

(Prov. 14:1)

It is fashionable these days to be a victim—of circumstances, environment, heredity, the "system"; take your pick. Whatever is wrong with us is someone else's fault. We lose our temper because we're Irish, German, Spanish, or Italian. We shoplift because our parents didn't give us enough allowance. We're fat because our husbands eat too much. Otherwise God is to blame.

One of our radio stations carries a weekly program in which a minister-counselor answers questions about marriage. Frequently a call will come in: "My husband has not given me a present or even a greeting card for eighteen years"; or "My daughter and her husband have refused to move out of our house for six years, and I think it's time they had their own place." The minister always asks the same question: "How much worse do things have to get before you will do something? How long will you suffer before you get help?"

The caller is surprised. She had never assumed any personal responsibility for the situation. While she was resentful and bitter, even hating the abuses, she tolerated them, hoping that tomorrow would somehow be better.

God has given us minds and bodies, and called us to build families. We have many means to help us with construction problems, including the wisdom of Scripture. We also have the counsel and fellowship of our church members. Christian problem solvers are available now in every profession—law, medicine, psychology, business. Above all is the power of the Holy Spirit, enabling us to change ourselves and our situations so that our families more clearly reflect God's image. A wise builder utilizes sub-contractors.

Whatever problem is disturbing your family, you do not have to watch it destroy relationships. Assume responsibility and get help.

Father, it's so easy to blame everyone else for what is wrong in my family. I need the power of your Holy Spirit to change myself. Enable me to admit my failings. Take away the pride that keeps me from getting help. Help me not to glorify needless suffering.

Power verses: Ephesians 1:13–15; 1 Corinthians 1:20–31.

> "Plans fail
> for lack of counsel,
> but with many advisors
> they succeed."
>
> (Prov. 15:22)

One of our children had made a major decision that grieved us deeply. My husband and I talked about it at length and arrived at what appeared to be a scriptural position. We asked our friends to pray for us as we approached a confrontation. One by one, they came to us, concerned about our decision. All of them were suggesting another plan. In the space of twelve hours we changed our minds, followed their advice, and saw God deepen our relationship with our child. Had we proceeded alone, the result would have been tragic.

Who can be objective when family is concerned? No parent sees a child through clear eyes. We are too harsh or too indulgent. We react out of our own experiences as children. Our feelings are colored by the state of our own marriages. We are subject to all the judgmental errors that beset human beings.

God has wisely and lovingly placed us in His church, surrounded by advisors who see us from a different perspective. When we share our problems and humble ourselves to admit we need support, they can counsel.

God has provided another means. In Psalm 119:24 we read, "Your statues are my delight; they are my counselors." God's law a delight? Yes, all of it is for our good. It was written to bring us joy. "Your statutes are my heritage forever; they are the joy of my heart" (Ps. 119:111).

Are you making plans right now? God does not expect you to act alone. He has provided His statutes and His people. When they agree with us, we can proceed, confident of success.

I'm independent, Lord. I like to make up my own mind. Give me a spirit of submission. Make me open to counsel from Christian friends. Lead me deeper into your Word. May I say with the psalmist, "Your statutes are wonderful; therefore I obey them" (Ps. 119:129).

The other side of good advice: Proverbs 15:23. ☕

> ## "Commit to the Lord
> ## whatever you do,
> ## and your plans
> ## will succeed."
>
> **(Prov. 16:3)**

Our usual order of commitment is to proceed with a project and dedicate it to the Lord when it's all finished. After we've bought the house and mortgaged ourselves into a two-wage existence for fifteen years, we say, "It's your tri-level, Lord. May it be used for your glory."

The proverb doesn't say, "Commit your plans to the Lord, and whatever you do will succeed." Before we even lift up a pen or a plumb line, we are to ask God whether He wants our idea discarded or set in motion. The question is not what choice to make, but whether or not we should choose.

Once our project is underway, we are to ask God repeatedly for instruction. Like a child running back to her parent for advice on how to do something, we keep checking with God. A Hebrew idiom says it beautifully: Roll it over on Jehovah.

At the moment our project is completed, it becomes an offering to the Lord. It is His vice-presidency, His car, or His loaf of home-baked bread. Our prayers have been answered. A new idea is fomenting, and the commitment process begins again, strengthened by the knowledge that when we consult God first, He promises wisdom.

I've got this fantastic idea, Lord, and I want to know what You think of it. Show me in your Word, and through Christian counsel, whether or not I should proceed.

Read Psalm 37 to find additional blessings from commitment to the Lord.

"Better a little with righteousness than much gain with injustice."

(Prov. 16:8)

Honesty at all costs is the theme here. The proverb is not speaking against wealth, but against the way it is acquired.

The poor but honest worker happily trudging home to his third-floor, walk-up apartment while his scoundrel of an employer chews antacid pills in the back seat of his Rolls Royce is largely a mythical creature dreamed up by some producer of religious films. To most people, a little is not better than much. And the person who has acquired wealth through unscrupulous means decides his life of luxury is well worth a little discomfort. Any discovered illegalities can be handled by his well-paid legal staff.

So why be honest? Why is it the best policy? Righteousness is the key. It is God's requirement for people so that they can exist in community with other people. Were wickedness to be the norm, the most wicked would enslave the rest of us. Genesis 6:10 describes such a condition: "Now the earth was corrupt in God's sight and was full of violence."

Righteousness allows me to live with myself and gives me a peaceful conscience. I am not a slave to my own sinful nature, vividly described by Paul in Galatians 5 as: sexual immorality, impurity and debauchery, idolatry and witchcraft, hatred, discord, jealousy, fits of rage, selfish ambition, dissensions, factions and envy, drunkenness, orgies, and the like.

Most important, righteousness lets me live with God, my creator and sustainer. I can comprehend, at least in some measure, His mind and will. This relationship ennobles me and lifts me out of the worthlessness, guilt, and anxiety which plagues all those without God, no matter what their material possessions. When I am at peace with God, I can live with a little food, a little house, a little wardrobe, and really find it to be better.

The temptation to be dishonest is everywhere. Help me, Lord, to resist even when my honesty is ridiculed by others. Make me content with what I have. May I rejoice in knowing You.

"Perks" are the little extras that come with a job. They can be free paper clips or a longer lunch hour. Have you taken advantage of your employer by helping yourself to more than your share? What about long coffee breaks? ☕

"Honest scales and balances are from the Lord; all the weights in the bag are of his making."

(Prov. 16:11)

Today weights and measures are determined by the National Bureau of Standards in Washington, D.C. But in the days of the Israelite kings, standardization was decreed by royal authority. The merchant who chipped down his stone weights to create a false balance, had to answer to the king. This proverb reminds us that authorization for scales and balances goes further back than that. God is concerned about even such humble matters as how much hamburger is really on the plastic meat tray. The scale that weighed it is His.

Unscrupulous merchants must have set up their booths as soon as the first family settled outside the garden of Eden. In the book of Leviticus, when God gave the Law to Moses, He says, "Do not use dishonest standards when measuring length, weight or quantity. Use honest scales and honest weights, an honest ephah [dry measure] and an honest hin [liquid measure]. I am the Lord your God, who brought you out of Egypt" (Lev. 19:35).

A consumer testing company opened up a fruit pie sold by a famous hamburger chain and found that it contained three cherries. The picture on the wrapper showed a filling chock-full of red fruit. A television commercial about soup achieved the effect of lots of meat and vegetables by placing marbles in the bottom of the bowl. A survey to determine the honesty of auto mechanics found that most of the work prescribed for an ailing engine was unnecessary; the malfunction could have been corrected by reattaching one wire.

It's so easy to misrepresent one's product. Everybody is in such a hurry these days that who notices a fraction of an ounce, a slight deviation from the advertisement? When this deception is promoted by the executive, is the employee who carries out the order responsible? After all, she's only doing what she's told; she's not being dishonest herself.

God's Word calls for honest merchandising. Christians must disengage themselves from shady practices. Assuming that their work has been productive, a calm but firm protest to the person in charge may be all that is necessary to bring matters right. If not, obedience to God's standard requires finding another job.

Lord, may my stone weights be exactly what I say they are. Keep me from chiseling.

Do you work for an honest company? Encourage your boss.

"How much better
to get wisdom than gold,
to choose understanding
rather than silver!"

(Prov. 16:16)

Considering the cost of a college education these days, and the price of gold, this proverb seems sadly out of touch with the times. The new high-school graduate might do better joining the resurgent California gold panners than going on to college.

We must distinguish between wisdom and knowledge. "Wisdom is the intelligent application of learning, the ability to discern inner qualities and essential relationships" (Websters Third New International Dictionary). Knowledge is an acquaintance with facts, truths and principles. A sixteen year-old girl may have the knowledge necessary to pass a driving test, but that doesn't mean she has the wisdom to handle the car properly in all situations. Even though she knows all the appropriate speed limits, she may drive when she's been drinking.

Wisdom and understanding equip a person to make good use of what talents she has. The woman with limited abilities who assesses them properly in the light of godly counsel will be more prosperous than the multi-talented individual who runs in all directions, never seeking God's will. A friend of mine who spent twenty years trying to be a supper-club entertainer has at last found peace and profit as a florist.

Jesus said that whoever heard His words and put them into practice was like a wise man who built his house upon a rock. When a great storm came, the house, because of its foundation, stood firm. Our strength is in our understanding and obedience to Scripture. Jesus commands us to seek first His kingdom and His righteousness, and all our needs will be supplied. Those who seek money and not wisdom suffer a double loss. They will never have wisdom, and will eventually lose their money. Those who seek wisdom and not money may enjoy a double gain. They will be given wisdom and may gain material satisfaction as well.

Father, lead me into a deeper study of your Word, that I may get wisdom. Give me an obedient spirit as I gain understanding of Jesus' teachings. Help me to put money in its proper perspective.

Meditate on this: When Christ is yours, all things are yours, including gold and silver.

"Pride goes
before destruction,
a haughty spirit
before a fall."

(Prov. 16:18)

We have a stereotype of a proud woman. She's a well-fed person, wearing a long dress. One hand holds the hoop of her train, and the other clasps a lorgnette through which she peers with slightly-veiled contempt. Since none of us really looks like that, we think that none of us is proud.

The Bible paints a different picture. A proud person is described in Psalm 10 not as one who has a special appearance, but as one who does not seek the Lord. "In all his thoughts there is no room for God." God's laws are far from him. He sneers at his enemies. He says to himself, "Nothing will shake me; I'll always be happy and never have trouble." One way he never has trouble is by bull-dozing over anyone who stands in his way.

Pride is a person's thinking he doesn't need God: "I'll make it on my own, thank you." Pride is never reading the Bible because of disbelief that it really has anything important to say. It takes humility to get up early every morning and study God's Word. Pride is also refusing to take counsel, whether it's from the pulpit, in a Bible class, or from a Christian friend who's come over for a cup of coffee. It's Frank Sinatra singing, "I did it my way."

Pride is a woman's sneering at her enemies, whether the enemy is a new person at church who thinks the women's society could be changed, or a neighbor who doesn't like someone else's basset hound digging up her tulips. Pride is never admitting any burdens, never shar-ing, and never totally opening up. The whole world may fall apart, but the proud woman won't let anyone know. She pretends everything is going just great. She's super Christian, isolated from others who are hurting.

The result of pride is clear: destruction. It may come through personal disaster in this life. It most certainly will come at death. "All the arrogant and every evil done will be stubble, and that day that is coming will set them on fire" (Mal. 4:1).

I think I'm pretty humble, Lord. Do you agree? Help me to see myself as you see me. If this means reading my Bible more thoroughly, awaken my interest.

Read for further insight: Romans 12:1–8. Write down what are your gifts and what are not your gifts. Ask a friend what she thinks. ☕

"Better to be lowly in spirit
and among the oppressed
than to share plunder
with the proud."

(Prov. 16:19)

How could it be better to be among the oppressed? Who would deliberately live with the refugees in Cambodia, or with the lower class in Haiti? Sharing plunder with the proud may not be a comfortable situation either, but it sure beats living with the oppressed.

And why is having a lowly spirit equated with oppression? Can't I be lowly in spirit and not suffer for it?

Jesus, who was the meekest and most lowly in heart of all men, frequently reminded His followers that those qualities would make them insulted, persecuted, and falsely accused of all kinds of evil. People who act like sheep can expect to be preyed upon by wolves.

The world is marked by pride, described in 1 John 2 as sinful cravings, lusting eyes, and boasting. It has no fear of the Lord, but thinks only of itself. The follower of Jesus is marked by humility, seeking to bring glory to God through love for others. Such an attitude reminds the world of its own sin, arousing its anger and inciting the devil himself. Yes, the woman lowly in spirit is a target for battle.

Then, what is better about being lowly? Ironically, even as the warfare continues, I have peace: peace with myself, as I am obedient to God; peace with my neighbor as I love her as myself; and peace with God as I love Him with all my heart, soul, mind, and strength. The proud of the world plunder and steal from each other. The spoils of war are never secure, as the person who is robbed today will rob back tomorrow.

Jesus promises the gentle and humble in heart rest for their souls. Having a soul at peace with God assures happiness anywhere, even among the oppressed.

"My heart is not proud, O Lord, my eyes are not haughty; I do not concern myself with great matters or things too wonderful for me. But I have stilled and quieted my soul; like a weaned child with its mother, like a weaned child is my soul within me" (Ps. 131:1–2).

What kind of plunder do the proud share?

"Whoever gives heed to
instruction prospers,
and blessed is he who
trusts in the Lord."

(Prov. 16:20)

When all else fails, read the directions," said my husband as he patiently pulled threads out of the jammed-up sewing machine. Over the years he has fixed blenders, washing machines, mixers, and everything else that has more than two moving parts.

Many people let their lives get all jammed up, and then, when all else fails, they read God's directions. In His mercy, He helps us get straightened out, but often a lifetime is needlessly spent in misery and despair. The thief on the cross came to Jesus in the final moment of his life. Praise God that it is never too late, but had he obeyed his Savior's teachings when he first heard them taught, he could have avoided a torturous and early death.

The woman who gives heed to God's instruction not only lives, but prospers. As she reads the Bible and trusts in the Lord to do what He says He will, He directs her life, making it more efficient and productive. Purpose replaces aimlessness; mistakes in judgment are minimized; and relationships improve. God does want the best for His people, and He has put together a most practical operating manual for them. But to be effective it has to be read.

Besides prosperity, God promises happiness. When we trust Him we are blessed, the Amplified Bible says, "with life-joy and satisfaction in God's favor and salvation, regardless of your outward conditions."

I would like to be prosperous and blessed, Father. Thank you for showing me how in your Word. Help me to read it faithfully, and do what it says.

Did you know that God also gives you a guarantee? Read John 8:51. ☕

"The wise in heart
are called discerning,
and pleasant words
promote instructions."

(Prov. 16:21)

Discernment is that peculiar aspect of wisdom which pairs judgment with understanding. The wise person sees the situation correctly, and responds with warm and encouraging speech. Anne observed that the minister's wife was working too hard. She called her on the phone and warned her about ruining her health. Stephanie observed that the minister's wife was working too hard. She took her to lunch and a matinee at symphony hall. Driving home after the concert, Stephanie was able to share some ideas for delegating responsibility to other women in the church.

Children also are the object of much unpleasant instruction. Grumpy adults quickly lose patience with two-year-olds who resist toilet training, six-year-olds who can't tie their own shoes, and sixteen-year-olds who want extra practice so they can get their driver's licenses. The ultimate test of patience is teaching parallel parking. Pleasant words are hard to come by when the youthful driver has the rear wheel up on the curb for the ninth time.

In almost every employment situation, someone new to the job must be trained. Sometimes this takes place in formal teaching sessions, but more likely the trainee is simply assigned to another employee: "This is Rose. She'll show you the ropes." The Christian who can cheerfully work with an apprentice, praising her for each step of progress, can make an indelible mark on that person's life. At a time of unusual anxiety, the heart is peculiarly open to the gospel. The pleasant instructor may find that the person in need of instruction also has a most teachable soul.

Some people are so dumb, Lord! I tell them over and over, and still they don't get it. Help me to remember my own struggles when I have to learn something. Give me pleasant words, not phony, but genuine, out of a loving spirit.

Encouragement is a gift. Read Romans 12:8. Do you have it? If you desire it, God will give it to you. Read 1 Corinthians 1:4–9.

"Pleasant words
are a honeycomb,
sweet to the soul and
healing to the bones."

(Prov. 16:24)

In his book, *None of These Diseases*, S. I. McMillen says, "The development of arthritis from fear and emotional disturbances is common. We do not understand the mechanism, but the fact of its occurrence is well known. Some people who are crippled for life in many of their joints give a clear-cut history of emotional stress" (p. 93). Dr. McMillen acknowledges that arthritis can be caused by fatigue, injury, or exposure to wet and cold, but he considers these merely as additional stress factors.

Our immediate response to this proverb may be a conviction to speak pleasantly to other people to relieve their stress. Sure, this is a proper action. But Dr. McMillen repeatedly draws our attention to the value of being pleasant for our own good. A sweet soul, free from hatred, resentment, jealousy, anger, and other negative emotions, affects the emotional center of the brain, which is intrinsically related to all the vital organs of our body. Who hasn't experienced a tension headache, or an upset stomach brought on by worry? Everyone knows the unpleasant effect that anxiety has on the intestines.

In his letter of Gaius the Elder, John writes, "Dear friend, I pray that you may enjoy good health and that all may go well with you, even as your soul is getting along well" (3 John:2). John knew how to have a well soul. He had worked intimately with Christ, and saw His healing power in the lives of those who believed Him to be their Savior.

To those who believe in Him, Jesus promises rest, joy, and peace. Emotional stress can be overcome, allowing the body to function at its best.

Dear Jesus, I claim your promise that those who love you will be given the power and ability to handle the emotional problems that come in this life. May I have pleasant feelings, Lord, and thus pleasant words. My bones do ache, and I long for healing.

"Stress does not affect everyone in the same way. Some people withstand stress better than others. But generally, people with arthritis can trace the start of their disease to an incident or a sequence of events that affected them deeply. Common among women in their middle years is the shock of losing their husband. This presents a threat to their security; they may feel that they cannot manage by themselves" (Understanding Arthritis, William Kitay, Monarch Press, 1977, p. 17).

"The laborer's appetite works for him; his hunger drives him on."

(Prov. 16:26)

Eddie was a healthy young man of nineteen who spent his first year out of high school listening to his stereo and repairing his car. His two best friends were a nineteen-inch, colored TV and a guy named Danny, who worked part-time in a bicycle store. The high school counselor said that Eddie had not yet "reached his full potential." His mother told her own mother that he hadn't "found himself yet." His sister, who went to college, said he was going through an identity crisis. His father told Eddie he was tired of having a lazy bum around the house all day and that at the beginning of the month, he was charging for room and board. Two days later, Eddie found a job.

Parents beset by unemployed children can find ample support in Scripture for refusing to feed and house them for nothing. Ephesians 4:28 says, "He who has been stealing, must steal no longer, but must work, doing something useful with his hands, that he may have something to share with those in need." Then there is the classic rule in 2 Thessalonians 3:10, "If a man will not work, he shall not eat."

Nor should the value of work be limited to grown children. Even pre-schoolers can be given daily responsibilities, such as emptying wastebaskets and setting the table. Sorting socks is excellent training for reading readiness. Caring for a pet relates consistent provision of food and water with the continuance of life. I know a mother once who actually meant it when she told her son and daughter that it they wanted to have a dog they had to take care of it. They didn't, and out went the dog to the humane society.

There is no need for an allowance. We don't get paid for being responsible members of our family. Such an incentive shouldn't be necessary. The promise of three meals a day will whet the laborer's appetite, driving him on to work. There is nothing like a little hunger to encourage industry.

Thank you, God, for giving me work to do. Many are unemployed today. Many see nothing useful to do at home. Help me to be a faithful worker. Supply my daily bread and give me the desire to share it.

Spend some time with each of your children, drawing up a list of responsibilities to be done. Can you be strong enough to deny an evening meal to the lazy ones? ☕

> "A perverse man
> stirs up dissensions,
> and a gossip separates
> close friends."
>
> **(Prov. 16:28)**

In Judges 15 we read how Samson caught three hundred foxes and tied them tail to tail in pairs. He then set the tails afire and let the foxes run through the Philistine grain fields. Everything growing there, including the vineyards and olive trees, burned up.

The same Hebrew word used to describe the spreading of fire from those foxes is the word used in this proverb, to describe the spread of dissension caused by a perverse person. Dissension is never static. Like fire in a grain field, it must either increase or be stamped out. This is because it comes from perverse people—stubborn, obstinate people opposed to what is reasonable. Dissension involves quarreling and loss of friends. Disagreement, on the other hand, is only a temporary difference which can be reconciled.

Another action which destroys friendship is gossip. A gossip can lose a friend by revealing personal information which she learned in trusting confidence. Or she can separate close friends by talking about one to the other. This may take the subtle form of "learning about someone so you can understand her better and pray more intelligently."

Both dissension and gossip are sins of the tongue. Both are wedges, dividing people who were once of common mind and interest. "Set a guard over my mouth, O Lord; keep watch over the door of my lips," David prayed (Ps. 141:3). He knew where harmful words originated, for he goes on to say, "Let not my heart be drawn to what is evil, to take part in wicked deeds with men who are evildoers; let me not eat of their delicacies" (Ps. 141:4).

Keep me away from people who will encourage me to say wicked things, Lord. May I not join in with dissenters and gossips. And wherever I am, Lord, help me to keep my mouth shut.

Are there dissensions within your church? What can you say that will help them to be reconciled? 🍵

> "Gray hair is a
> crown of splendor;
> it is attained by
> a righteous life."
>
> (Prov. 16:31)

My immediate reaction to this proverb was, "Aw, come on!" There are many unrighteous people walking around with gray hair, flaunting their wickedness on everything from porno magazines to TV newscasts. Conversely, many a Christian in her fifties sports a head of flaming red or jet black—pick your color. Unless men stop aging when they become employed on TV news shows, they too apparently find nothing wrong with a little touch-up. Don't they want a crown of splendor?

The point here is attitude. So you look in the mirror one morning and see your first gray hair. You've been taking all the right vitamins, and still that tell-tale sign of aging is there. You pluck it out, but next week there are three gray hairs, and then your hairdresser says, "How about a rinse, Ms. Jenkins? Just a little color to pick up the highlights."

You are getting old. It shows up in your skin, and that slight bulge in the tummy, but the most obvious sign is the graying hair. God uses it to remind us that life is, indeed, temporary. None of us goes on forever, no matter how we can conceal the aging process. Life is a gift from God, to be taken back when He determines.

We can regard age as a blessing. God has allowed us these extra years to praise His name, to serve others, to enjoy the evidences of His goodness to us. We can wear our gray hair with humble thanksgiving. Millions throughout the world never live long enough to be old. In our country vigorous life after seventy is not uncommon.

Does a righteous life really help us to live longer? In Proverbs 3:2 we read that when we obey God's teaching He promises us a long and prosperous life. First, we avoid the violence of wickedness. Secondly, when we follow the Bible's wisdom in our society, we care for each other's individual needs.

How beautiful is gray hair. It is a sign of God's blessing, whether we acknowledge it or not.

Father, whether I cover up the gray or leave it alone, it's still there. Help me to accept my age. Help me even to thank you for it. May I use my days for your glory, doing what good I can, while there is still time.

What about hair dye? What difference would it make in your life if you stopped using it? Or started? 🍵

> ## "Better a dry crust
> ## with peace and quiet
> ## than a house
> ## full of feasting,
> ## with strife."
>
> **(Prov. 17:1)**

Feasting was a prescribed activity of Old Testament Jewish religion. One example was the family feast with its peace offering, such as observed by Elkanah, with his wives Hannah and Peninnah. There were also national feasts which thousands attended to offer sacrifices and bring their tithes and special gifts. The people were to "rejoice before the Lord" (Deut. 12:12).

Rather than a religious observance, church feasting today falls more into the category of "fun, food, and fellowship." There is always plenty of food, and usually some fellowship. Fun is harder to come by.

The planning committee is split on the issue of an organized potluck versus a true "leave it to Providence," which might result in seven coleslaws and no mostaccioli. The deacons don't see why setting up the tables is *their* job. The M.C. threatens to resign if *anybody* sings even one note from "Sound of Music." At 11:22, when the last soggy dish towel has been hung over the kitchen sink, the clean-up crew is not too happy, either. Truly, there can be much strife in the Lord's house when it is full of feasting.

Inviting the congregation to a meal of dry crusts, even with peace and quiet, is not too appealing. By using such contrast the proverb writer forces us to reconsider our objectives in planning church feasts. The goal of sharing with believers to the mutual benefit of all must be kept clearly in mind. Individual preferences have to be considered, but never to the detriment of the body of Christ. Considerable yielding is necessary on all sides.

As we sit shoulder-to-shoulder in the pew during worship, it is comparitively easy to feel peaceful. The test comes when we leave the sanctuary and become involved in church activity. Whether this is a battlefield or a beatitude depends upon our willingness to see the church as a household of God, in which we are family members.

I think of myself as a good church worker, Lord. Am I strong-willed and troublesome? Do I complain? Give me love for others in my church. Help me to appreciate their efforts. Make our church a house that is known for its peace and quiet.

Tradition can make an original idea into a dreaded burden. Perhaps it is time to reassess your church dinners and either change their format or eliminate those that have lost their original purpose. ☕

"The crucible for silver
and the furnace for gold,
but the Lord tests
the heart."

(Prov. 17:3)

The test of an ore is in the crucible, where the pure metal collects after it has been heated to an extremely high temperature. The test of a person is her heart, the sum total of her mind, will, and emotions. God respects appearance and work, but His first interest is in character.

This He subjects to various trials or tests, so that it may be cleansed of impurities.

The picture of God as a tester conjures up, for some people, the image of a harsh teacher—the kind who purposely designs tests so that half the class fails. Others see God putting us through difficult times to "teach us a lesson," like the mother who lets her child get burned on a hot stove so he won't touch it next time. Then there is the view of God as an examiner like the one at the Department of Motor Vehicles. He sits with us in the front seat of life, and tells us to make left and right turns while He grades our performance.

God's tests are never destructive. It is not His desire that we should fail, or be hurt, or humiliated, Rather, He accompanies us when we are under trial and helps to sort out the precious experience from that which is worthless. Our discernment for righteousness grows. In the choices of life, God wants us to choose correctly.

Father, I've been to school, and I know that without tests I'd never be motivated to learn anything. Thank you for my trials which teach me to choose what is best for me. Refine me, that I may be purged of impurities.

Are you going through a hard time right now? What is God lovingly trying to teach you? From this experience, what new choices will you make? ☕

"He who mocks the poor
shows contempt for their Maker;
whoever gloats over disaster
will not go unpunished."

(Prov. 17:5)

Every time a famine wipes out millions in India, at least one Christian will say, "Well, that's what they get for being Hindus. They deserve God's punishment. If they ate all those cows roaming through the streets, they wouldn't be so hungry."

Closer to home, we have people who condemn everyone on welfare as being sneaky and shiftless. Never mind whether these people are sick, illiterate, emotionally broken, or the victims of myriad circumstances that have piled up year after year. Someone will say, "Anybody who wants to work can find a job."

Jesus took a far different attitude toward the poor. In Matthew 25 He equates the evidence of our salvation with our work for the less fortunate. If we really love Jesus, we will be feeding and clothing the poor, offering hospitality to strangers, and visiting prisoners. Rather than being burdens to society, these people are blessed opportunities for us to minister to Christ Himself.

Jesus took the doctrine of creation seriously. God made the poor, and any contempt we show for them is contempt for God. Such arrogance will not go unpunished. Christians should be actively working to alleviate poverty, and restore those in need, but always with an attitude of humility. Our own present state of well-being is not due to our own efforts, but results from God's grace.

Lord Jesus, for our sakes You became poor, that we might become rich. Give me a generous heart. Make me glad to share what I have. Forgive me for my hasty conclusions about those on welfare and in prison. How little I know about their situation!

A suburban church stopped collecting money for the poor, because it didn't know any poor people. Can you list at least five men or women who could benefit from your concern and money? ☕

> ## "Children's children are a crown to the aged, and parents are the pride of their children."
>
> (Prov. 17:6)

How are your grandchildren?" is a question that usually produces a wallet full of pictures. Visit anyone over fifty, and notice how many photographs are on the mantle, the end table, the piano, and the walls. Truly, the elderly delight in their grandchildren and rejoice in their accomplishments.

Children and grandchildren are to delight in the accomplishments of their aged relatives. This may take the form of grateful reflection for all they did for us when we were young. (We must remember that whatever mistakes they made in child-rearing, we were not the easiest children to raise.) It usually takes years for us to appreciate their efforts. During my teens when I was going to be an airplane pilot, and then a buyer of high fashion in a department store, my mother gave me opportunities to speak before church groups and encouraged me to write. Her persistent encouragement was not always accepted graciously, but I look back now and see how the Lord used her to prepare me for what I enjoy doing most.

We can take pride in whatever grandmother and grandfather are doing today. They may be spending their retirement years on a mission field, joining hundreds of other senior citizens whose potential for service has at last been recognized. For others, accomplishment may be forcing a reluctant body to walk to the dining room for dinner, or continuing to write letters when the fingers throb with arthritic pain.

Each of us is but a link in a human chain that binds one generation to the next. It is humbling to realize how much of what we are came from our parents. We must also realize that we are determining through our lives what our children will be like. As the years go by, will they have reason to be proud of us?

Lord God, help me to see the good in my children and in my parents. Open my mouth to say words of encouragement and praise.

Get out that box of old photographs, and look them over again in an attitude of praise and prayer. ☕

"He who covers over an
offense promotes love,
but whoever repeats the matter
separates close friends."

(Prov. 17:9)

Claire walked into the church kitchen with two bags
of groceries, and wondered just where she could set them
down. Dirty coffee cups and salad plates covered the
counter and filled the sink. A cold coffee urn, still holding
its basket of soggy grounds, stood on the pass-through.
What a mess!

It was two-thirty in the afternoon, long past the noon-
hour Bible study. Claire checked the kitchen schedule to
see who was in charge. Laura Dillart. Wouldn't you know!

Laura had the messiest house in the congregation. Evidently she felt right at home in church.

Nothing to do but clean up. The spaghetti sauce had to be on by three, and Margaret wouldn't be coming to help until three-thirty. Claire set the bags on the floor and quickly loaded the dishwasher. With speed and determination she cleaned the urn and wiped the counters while the hamburger browned in the electric oven.

When Margaret arrived the spaghetti sauce was simmering, its aroma just beginning to permeate the fellowship hall. "Well, I see you've got everything under control," she said, setting her box of supplies on the sparkling-clean table top. Claire just nodded. No point in saying anything about Laura. The last person she needed to irritate was Margaret, who even cleaned her potting soil. After years of contention the two women were finally beginning to appreciate each other.

It was four-thirty and Margaret had left to buy coffee cream. Claire was buttering the garlic bread when Laura came flying into the kitchen, coat half-buttoned as usual. "Oh Claire," she cried, "I'm so sorry about the kitchen! I was just starting to clean up when I got a call from school that Jim had dislocated his shoulder in gym class. Had to take him to the emergency ward and then home. Did we have a time! Poor kid was in terrible pain!"

"I'm glad you were able to be with him, Laura. It didn't take me long to clean the kitchen, so don't give it another thought." Margaret appeared with the cream. "Hi, Laura. What brings you here?"

"She just stopped in to see how we were doing," Claire said quickly. The smile she got from Laura more than made up for the dirty dishes.

Gossip is fun, Lord. Help me to hate it.

Two more thoughts on gossip: Proverbs 16:28 and 20:19.

"Starting a quarrel
is like breaching a dam;
so drop the matter
before a dispute breaks out."

(Prov. 17:14)

Hi and Lois, popular comic characters, are sitting at the table when they hear, "Ditto! You dumb little twerp! I'm gonna smash you! Stay outa my stuff, you little crumb!" Hi calls out, "Chip!" Then he hears, "You make one move and I'll throw you right out the front door!" "Chip!" Hi calls out again. "Chip, please come in here! What's going on between you and Ditto?" Chip appears in the doorway and explains, "Personal differences." Hi turns to Lois and says, "For a while there I thought they were fighting."

Nobody quarrels anymore. People have disputes, confrontations, or differences of opinion. In our family we have "vehement discussions." Call them what you will, when anger is present, there is a break in the relationship between the opposing parties. Like a crack in a dam, cruel words gush out, and we cannot predict, control, or retrieve them. The result is deep, long-lasting hurt.

The Bible tells us not to start a quarrel. "Drop the matter before a dispute breaks out" (Prov. 17:14). But how? Even if I control my tongue, the anger is still there, ready to spill out somewhere else. Bottled up, the same anger gives me a headache, or high blood pressure, or poor digestion.

Scripture offers help. We are to: realize that anger is sinful (Gal. 5:19); be led by the Holy Spirit to love and serve others (Gal. 5:16–18); and pray (1 Tim. 2:8). Of immediate practical value is James 1:19: "Be quick to listen, slow to speak and slow to become angry." How many quarrels would be prevented if we would really listen to the other person, not only for the content of her grievance, but also for the feelings in her heart which prompt it? Free of the need to defend ourselves, we can give the matter thoughtful attention. We may even be led to agree. That is one sure way to drop the matter.

Heavenly Father, take away my pride, which makes me want to appear right in every situation. Help me to appreciate other points of view. And Father, in matters of little importance, give me the extraordinary power to say nothing.

For the next two weeks, keep a list of situations in which you quarrel. Is there a pattern? Do you see certain irritations cropping up over and over again? Pray specifically about these.

"Of what use is money in the hand of a fool, since he has no desire to get wisdom?"

(Prov. 17:16)

A friend of mine has a son who received his first car when he was fifteen. Even though he was too young to drive it, he had the satisfaction of owning it, thus being equal to his friends. The day after his sixteenth birthday, he passed his driver's test, thus enabling him to drive it half a mile to school. Three weeks later he got his first citation for speeding.

Maintaining the car and buying gasoline necessitated getting a job in a fast-food restaurant. While the boy was busy French-frying potatoes, he neglected his school work. His first post-car report card showed three C's and two D's. His parents took the car away, which meant that their son had to quit his job. They had to take over the payments on his new stereo.

It is not mental deficiency which makes a person a fool. Rather, it is his inability to make sensible judgments. God calls us to base all of life's decisions upon the wisdom of His word. In the matter of money, the Bible has much to say about how it should be earned, and how it should be spent. Faithful adherence to biblical principles promises prosperity. Jesus said, "Give, and it will be given to you. A good measure, pressed down, shaken together and running over, will be poured into your lap. For with the measure you use, it will be measured to you" (Luke 6:38).

Lord Jesus, there are times when my lap is very empty. Forgive me for being foolish with money. Give me the desire to get wisdom. I know this will mean a change in the way I live.

For further study on the use of money, read: 1 Timothy 6:17–21: Deuteronomy 8; 1 Peter 4:10; and Luke 16:10–13.

"A friend loves
at all times, and
a brother is born
for adversity."

(Prov. 17:17)

Judy thought the people in her apartment house were her friends, until she was attacked in the front hall. Her screams for help brought no one to her defense. The neighbors didn't want to get involved. When Judy finally got to a telephone, she called her sister, who promptly took her to the hospital and the police station. Then she took her home with her for the night.

When trouble comes, we realize the strength of family ties. Mother cares for the pregnant teen-ager; father loans money during the strike; brothers and sisters baby-sit, help with remodeling projects, or loan a car. It is the family which faithfully visits grandpa in the hospital, rearranging their schedules so he has company every day.

In adversity, we also experience the love of true friends. They come with their chicken casseroles, words of encouragement, and offers to do whatever is helpful. They pray for us. They listen to us. They make us a pot of tea at two in the morning.

How precious are those relatives and friends who love us in the bad times as well as the good ones. With the writer of Ecclesiastes we can say, "Two are better than one, because they have a good return for their work: If one falls down, his friend can help him up. But pity the man who falls down and has no one to help him up! Also, if two lie down together they can keep warm. But how can one keep warm alone?" (Eccl. 4:9–11).

Thank you, Lord, for those who love me all the time. Bless them with a greater awareness of your love. And Lord, may I be a friend who loves at all times, and a family member who can be depended upon in adversity.

Think of someone you know who is suffering today. Let her know of your concern in one definite, practical way.
There is a Friend who will never fail us: Romans 8:38–39.

"He who loves
a quarrel loves sin;
he who builds a high gate
invites destruction."

(Prov. 17:19)

At first reading, the two parts of this proverb seem to make no sense at all. What does loving a quarrel have to do with building a gate?

The subject here is arrogance, that attitude that a person is so important and successful that he can do what he pleases; the attitude that his money, social connections, position in the company, or office in the church protect him from the authority of God. Thus we have the choir director who resists any effort to change the church music program, the rich donor to the college who insists that her money be spent her way.

Arrogance can find expression in big events, such as one nation forcing its government upon another. But it can also be felt in such little ways as the bigger brother destroying the smaller brother's parking garage made out of blocks, for no other reason except he doesn't want him to enjoy it. The little brother's anguish and the quarrel that follow are part of the fun for the big brother. Many a child has rejoiced in the torment he caused, even as he is punished.

Adults are sometimes no better than little boys. Yesterday I heard a son describe his father, a well-known minister, as a "man who loves a good fight."

During the reign of King Hezekiah, there was a steward named Shebna who considered himself so important that he built an imposing sepulcher. God took note of his arrogance and told him he would roll him up tightly like a ball and throw him into a large country (Isa. 22:17–18).

We cannot protect ourselves from God's judgment. No matter how important we may think we are, in His eyes we are but balls to be tossed about by His power. Rich women, well-known ministers, and little boys, take note.

Lord Jesus, it is easy to use power for my own benefit. Satan always tempts me to feel important. You understand this, for he tempted you, too. Give me a humble spirit. Help me to direct all glory to you.

Can there be such a thing as a good fight? How would this differ from a sinful quarrel? Read 1 Timothy 6:11–12; 2 Timothy 4:6–8; and Hebrews 10:19–39. ☕

> **"A cheerful heart
> is good medicine,
> but a crushed spirit
> dries up the bones."**
>
> (Prov. 17:22)

Everyone has suffered from a crushed spirit. Father arrives home from work, absolutely defeated. Not one thing went right all day. Mother had a conference with the school counselor, and learned that Eddie is failing third grade. Janet doesn't make the cheerleading squad. Bill tells Louise he doesn't love her anymore. Shirley feels depressed and doesn't know why. Life has lost all its flavor.

In personal distress, no one wants her particular grief to be taken lightly. To Janet, not making the cheerleading squad is loss of esteem and defeat after weeks of practice. No, it's not the end of the world, but it is the end of Janet's world as far as high school is concerned. Louise will reflect later that Bill was not the best man for her, but right now she thinks no one will ever love her again.

Note that the cheerful heart called for in these situations belongs to the one crushed. Good medicine must be swallowed by the sick person herself. Healing does not take place by others in the family behaving with excessive cheerfulness, making jokes or dancing around the kitchen. Rather, their role is one of sympathy and encouragement, offering further support through prayer.

During times of dried bones, atmosphere can actually deter depression. A cheerful setting can be deliberately constructed to ease times of stress. Bright colors, music, a pretty dinner table, parsley garnish on the macaroni and cheese, a warm smile, all blend together to make home a happy place. The office outfitted with colorful furniture and a lush Swedish ivy help to make business more pleasant.

Whatever the environment, there must be a witness who can lead the crushed spirit to see Jesus as the true joy who can heal the diseased nature. "If you obey my commands, you will remain in my love," He says in John 15:10. "I have told you this so that my joy may be in you and that your joy may be complete" (John 15:11). This is the best medicine to restore the crushed spirit.

Lord Jesus, when I am going through hard times, I think more and more about myself and less about You. Forgive me. Lead me to your Word and its promises of joy in spite of affliction. Enable me to encourage others with a cheerful word.

Prescription for a depressed heart: Take one dose each day. Repeat as necessary. John 15:1–8, 9–17; 16:17–24; Ephesians 5:15–20; Psalm 16:5–11; Romans 5:1–5; Romans 15:13; Psalm 5.

> ## "A foolish son brings grief to his father and bitterness to the one who bore him."
>
> **(Prov. 17:25)**

How did the prodigal son's mother feel? Was she bitter? When she looked out the kitchen window and saw him coming down the road, did she run outside right behind her husband and give her son a big hug? Or did she say, "That ungrateful child! After all I've done for him, he goes off and lives like some hippy bum! Well, he can fool his father, but I've had it. That's the last time I'm going to put myself out for him!"

Foolish children present a dilemma. Should we repair the damage caused by the sin, or should we say, "You're on your own now. Don't expect me to care for your baby, pay your bills, or pay the fine." When is a gift of a hundred dollars the essential encouragement to persevere through a tough situation, and when is it another excuse not to become responsible?

We consider attitude before action. God makes no allowance for bitterness, telling us in Ephesians 4:31 to get rid of it, along with rage, anger, brawling, slander, and every other form of malice. We are to be kind and compassionate, forgiving as Christ forgave us. We cannot make a wise decision when we are filled with negative feelings about another person, particularly our own child.

We seek counsel from other Christians. Parents are notorious for their lack of objectivity in evaluating their children. Our pastor, elder, and Christian friends can bring the insight we lack. They can help us to examine our motives. Any of us can fall prey to that pathological joy of being needed which prompts us to perpetuate a relationship in which the other person is kept helpless.

We meditate upon God's word. Psalm 104:34 tells us this is pleasing to God. Older Biblical translations say that this is sweet when accompanied by joy in the Lord.

Dear God, take away any bitterness in my heart, especially toward my own children. Help me to restore broken relationships. Give me wisdom in parenting, in specific ways with my adult sons and daughters.

Take one of your children to lunch today. ☕

"A man of knowledge
uses words with restraint,
and a man of understanding
is even-tempered."

(Prov. 17:27)

The hardest thing about knowing a lot is keeping it to myself. If someone asks me a simple question in my chosen field of expertise, I want to give her two or three chapters of technical information. When my new daughter-in-law calls me on Sunday morning to find out how much water to put with the pot roast, she doesn't need a twenty-minute lesson on slow cookery.

People with much formal education have a way of intimidating those with lesser training. The graciousness to accept another person's limited knowledge, when you could spout off ten times as much, is a mark of Christian love, for it requires demeaning oneself so that the other person feels more valuable. This applies when your first grader makes you stop what you're doing while she triumphantly reads every page of her first primer. It has no less importance as your dinner guest offers you advice on how to raise African violets. You can accept her information without revealing all that you learned in your ten-week course at the botanical gardens.

Understanding how something, or someone, operates, should bring with it a calm spirit. No need to flare up and kick the vacuum cleaner when it doesn't work if you know enough to see that the hose is clogged or the bag is full. No need to spank Martha for spilling her milk if you appreciate the limited motor-coordination of four-year-olds.

"Words from a wise man's mouth are gracious," says Ecclesiastes 10:12. We who claim Christ as Lord and Savior cannot separate facts in the head from love in the heart.

Lord God, help me not to talk so much. Help me to listen more and rejoice in what other people know. Give me a genuine enthusiasm for those who have just learned something and have to share it with me.

A fool who holds his tongue is no longer a complete fool.

"A fool finds no pleasure
in understanding
but delights in airing
his own opinions."

(Prov. 18:2)

The fool enjoys ignorance. You can make her sit down and teach her something, but she won't like it. I have been a fool. I have received much valuable instruction in my life that I did not enjoy. It is disconcerting to be a mechanical klutz who has to learn from a ten-year-old how to operate a lawn mower. I took no pleasure at all in understanding the American economic system and then realizing that most of what I had believed was wrong. The day my pastor helped me to see how my arrogant attitude was disrupting the church was most painful.

While there is a certain kind of weird pleasure in being ignorant, there is a synonymous delight in expressing it. It is always possible to find someone who knows less, who can be awed by sheer verbosity, even though it is meaningless. Since one characteristic of being a fool is not knowing you are one, you feel able to express yourself on every issue. Television talk shows turn out these types in abundance. The current rage is the nutrition-diet-health expert who has never been in a science class or lab of any kind, but has just written a book.

In matters of religion, we are to be especially careful. When dealing with souls, we are to steer clear of mere opinions. It is the true Word of God we are to delight in and share. "Your statutes are my delight; they are my counselors," says the psalmist in 119:24.

Heavenly Father, forgive me for being stubborn and proud. Humble me so that I may learn from others and from You. Keep me from liking my opinions too much.

Write down six beliefs you are especially excited about. Which are facts, and which are opinions? ☕

"One who is slack
in his work
is brother to one
who destroys."

(Prov. 18:9)

Irresponsibility is one of the most irritating character faults. It rarely affects only the person who didn't do what he was supposed to. Somebody else's work is almost always impeded, leading to a chain of negative events. When I spend too much time visiting with a friend and get dinner started late, my husband has to rush off to his meeting without sufficient relaxation or preparation. His judgments are then not made from the best mental attitude, which may result in poor decisions. To recall an old adage, "For the want of a nail, . . . a war was lost."

To say that irresponsibility destroys may seem too harsh, but it can ruin a business, break up a family, or even lead to a policy decision which wrecks a church or a life. A church secretary forgot to write a ministerial candidate that the position had been given to someone else; while he was waiting to hear, he lost the opportunity to take another job. Sloppy teaching in a high school algebra class affected the score on a scholastic aptitude test and kept a student out of her preferred college. A salesman lost an important contract because his wife forgot to put gas in the tank of their car. By the time he found a station that was open, his client had bought the product from someone else.

Sure, we all forget once in a while. For these momentary lapses, forgiveness is the most appreciated of all Christian graces. Continual slackness, however, cannot be sloughed off with an "I'm so sorry." The root of the problem is really selfishness—not regarding the other person's business as important. In 1 Corinthians 10:24, Paul says "Nobody should seek his own good, but the good of others." When that perspective is firmly grasped, irresponsibility can be confessed and corrected.

Lord, I don't want to destroy anyone. Help me to promise only what I can do well, and then help me to keep my promise. Make me a careful worker, mindful of all the lives I am affecting by my laborers.

Begin each day with prayer, planning, and a pencil. Ask for guidance. Keeping in mind the last activity of the day, plan backwards. Write down all the necessary information for each thing you are going to do. ☕

"He who answers before listening— that is his folly and his shame."

(Prov. 18:13)

Our family has supper together every Sunday night after church. For two hours we engage in "over-lapping," beginning a sentence before the other person is finished. We get twice as much said that way (we think). We also do half as much listening. Then we have to phone each other during the week and get all the details we missed.

Listening is an art. There are actually seminars to teach people how to listen. The objective is not only to hear words, but also to hear the person behind them. I once had a neighbor who talked to me on the phone about the most trivial matters. What she was really saying was, "I'm lonely and bored. My husband is gone all the time, and I'm desperate for companionship."

One day a child came home from school and completely surprised her mother by asking why Mommy and Daddy hadn't gone to a party for a long time. Probing deeper into the question, the mother learned that a boy at school had discussed his parents' impending divorce at the lunch table that day. One reason he knew they were not getting along was the fact that they never went out together. The mother, who was a good listener, was able to reassure her child that she had no reason to be anxious about her own father and mother. Their social life was only taking a much-needed rest.

Answering before listening is the special snare of the self-important. It indicates a person so involved with her own thoughts and ideas that she is thinking about them, even while the other person is sharing hers. Haven't we all been victims of the glassy stare, indicating that the person to whom we're talking is mentally thousands of miles away, not hearing one word we're saying?

One time my husband came home from work and started to tell me all about a traumatic meeting he had attended. Right in the middle I interrupted, "Did you leave the car out? I have to go to the library." He walked out of the kitchen, leaving me with a half-mixed meat loaf, a half-told story, and a well-deserved feeling of shame.

God, I'm always asking you to help me to keep my mouth shut. Help me to open my ears. Going deeper, help me to listen behind the words and hear the heart.

For further thought: James 1:19–26.

> **"A man's spirit sustains
> him in sickness,
> but a crushed spirit
> who can bear?"**
>
> (Prov. 18:14)

Last week Mary Anne and I visited Helen in the hospital. She was awaiting an operation for intestinal cancer. We found her sitting on her bed, hooked up to a bottle of dietary supplement that ran through a tube in her nose.

A woman with attractive features anyway, she actually

looked lovely. She was wearing a smartly styled wig, just the right amount of make-up, and a pale blue robe. One of the marvels about Helen was the way she always looked pretty. For three years her cancer progressed, but she always kept up her appearance.

Most commendable was Helen's attitude. She was interested in other people, accepted invitations to social events, and had a positive attitude about a prognosis that couldn't be honestly hopeful. Even while she was dying, Helen was living. What sustained her? She gave all the credit to Jesus Christ, her Lord and Savior. His grace was sufficient for her, and His strength was made perfect in her weakness (2 Cor. 12:9).

Of course, Helen still got depressed. Coping with pain, treatments, increased weakness, brought on great discouragement and frustration. Her husband had died five years before, and she was concerned for her teen-age son. A conscientious housekeeper, she wanted her home to be picture-perfect. Some days she couldn't do anything but lie in bed.

And yet Helen's spirit was never crushed. It was tied to Jesus, and from Him she received the spiritual nourishment she needed, just like the tube through her nose. "He gives strength to the weary and increases the power of the weak" (Isa. 40:29).

Dear Jesus, I thank you for your Spirit. I could not bear the troubles of this life without you. Give me opportunity to share the reality of your power with someone who is suffering today.

"Short of outward resources, life is hard; short of inward, it is insupportable" (Derek Kidner).

"A gift opens the way
for the giver
and ushers him into
the presence of the great."

(Prov. 18:16)

People give gifts for many reasons. Jacob sent over 550 animals to pacify Esau, the brother he had deceived. When he was an old man, Jacob sent balm, honey, spices, and nuts to the lord over the land, so that he would let Judah and Benjamin come back home. David took ten cheeses to the captain of the army to sustain him in his fight against the Philistines. David later received from Abigail enough food to feed his army, to dissuade him from slaying her entire household.

A true gift is given voluntarily, with no expectation of a favor in return. It must be distinguished from a bribe—

difficult to do in these days when everything from ballpoint pens to cruises in the Bahamas are used to buy special consideration. "No strings attached" is a condition not easy to believe.

Certain occasions, like Christmas, birthdays, anniversaries, and bridal showers, require a gift. It is fun to open a present and decipher what the giver was thinking when she purchased it. While I was in graduate school, I received from my six-year-old daughter a neatly hemmed square of calico on which were embroidered the words, "Home, Stay Home." That was a jolting reminder of my unbalanced life.

Best of all is the love gift that comes as a complete surprise. Last January I found a bag of white narcissus bulbs on my doorstep. Mary Anne had left them to "brighten up my winter days."

We will probably never have occasion to be ushered into the presence of a great person like a king or the president of the United States. Our gifts go to the relatively unknown. A loaf of bread to a new neighbor begins a rich friendship. A book to a child prepares her heart for the gospel. Giving an elderly friend a ride to the supermarket lessens her isolation and provides her with an opportunity to share all she knows about growing roses. When we proceed from a generous heart we discover that great people are not found on thrones or in capitals, but right in our own block.

Dear Father, you know all about gifts, for you gave us your son, Jesus. And you have given me the whole world besides, with all its treasures. Thank you. Lead me to someone who will be blessed by something I have to give.

Think of something you already own which could make someone else happy. Make a love gift of it today. ☕

> "The first to present
> his case seems right,
> till another comes forward
> and questions him."
>
> (Prov. 18:17)

General Saul had done almost everything right. Following the Lord's instructions, he developed a clever battle plan that spared the friendly Kenites, and wiped out the hostile Amalekites. Everything that was despised and weak was totally destroyed. If successful wars were rated from one to ten, Saul had a solid nine.

But God had said to totally destroy, and Saul had spared King Agag and the best of the sheep and cattle. He meant well, he said. Agag was brought back as a special prize, and the animals were to be sacrificed to God at Gilgal. You can't fault a man for religiosity like that.

But God did find fault, and through the prophet Samuel, He rejected Saul as king over Israel. Saul's deceitfulness cost him his kingdom.

How easily we fool ourselves. We justify our actions and feel quite comfortable, until someone comes along and questions what we are doing. Put me in a garden center and I can fill up the station wagon with things that I "need." Put me at a missionary conference, and I haven't any money. If I came out of the garden center and met a missionary, I would be very apologetic.

The proverb warns us against forming hasty opinions about others. Jody's account of how she was unfairly treated at the Sunday School party takes a different perspective when the teacher explains his point of view. (It's a good thing I talked to the teacher before calling the minister.) According to your neighbor, it was your son who left the gate of his dog pen open. The boy was wearing a green sweatshirt, and doesn't your son own one? (Careless, forgetful boy—wait until I get my hands on him!) But he explains that he was down at the ball field all afternoon. Doesn't Rick Greenwald own a green shirt too? Forgive me, son, for assuming the worst.

I must listen to both sides of the story: (1) when justifying my own actions being questioned by another; (2) when questioning the actions of others who justify themselves.

Father God, make me quick to listen, slow to speak, and slow to become angry (James 1:19).

False judgment is one of the most common family problems. Make it a regular matter of discussion and prayer in your own home. 🍵

"He who finds a wife finds what is good and receives favor from the Lord."

(Prov. 18:22)

An examination of this verse fifteen years ago would have articulated all the Scripture passages on the qualities of a good wife. Today we appreciate its emphasis upon a man finding a wife, instead of some other kind of female associate. Sexual liaisons between unmarried people are so common today that we give them scant attention. It takes a million-dollar lawsuit between a Hollywood actor and his live-in sweetheart to arouse our interest.

The Lord's favor rests upon the man who finds a wife—a woman joined to him by marriage. No other arrangement receives God's approval. There are religious people—some who take the name Christian—who believe other variations are permissible. A girl of sixteen was seduced by a man who used portions of Genesis as support for their sexual relationship. More than one minister has been led from counseling a distraught woman in his congregation, to sleeping with her. God says a man is to find a *wife*.

This wife is more than a woman joined by marriage. Husband and wife can live together and have less in common than a waitress and a bus boy who work in the same restaurant. The marriage relationship spoken of in Scripture is not grabbing a glass of orange juice on the way to work in the morning, and using the same toothpaste before jumping into bed at night. It is the oneness of body and mind known to those who share a commitment to Jesus Christ. That means mutual dependency and submission. As the marriage matures, there is greater awareness of the uniqueness of the other person. This kind of relationship takes time and work. When other activities compete, they have to be set aside.

A good wife is first of all a good person—good in the sense of righteous through the blood of Christ. As her love for Christ increases, fed by His Word, nurtured through His church, so will her love for her husband.

Dear Lord, it is not easy to be a good wife. There are days when having a husband is irritating and miserable. Empower me by your Spirit to live wholeheartedly. Empower my husband to love me the same way. Help us to grow together in our love for your Son.

Can you rearrange your schedule so that you and your husband have some time to talk together? Could you take a short walk before dinner, or share a cup of tea before going to bed? ☕

"A man of many companions
may come to ruin,
but there is a friend
who sticks closer
than a brother."

(Prov. 18:24)

When Leslie came to live with us, we didn't know she was an alcoholic. We had accepted her from the psychiatric ward of a nearby hospital as an out-patient "for two weeks, until she finds an apartment." It was five months before she left—five months of drunkenness, depression, black-outs, hallucinations, disappearances, and emotional trauma that taxed our family to its limit.

Leslie would call from a bar and tease us by not giving its location. She had met some friends, and they had offered to buy her a drink. When she had money, she, in turn, was an "old friend" buying liquor for others. One night I found her in a restaurant, drinking with some former neighbors. In my rage and frustration, I told them just what I thought of such "friends." They knew she was an alcoholic. They led her into drinking, and actually enjoyed her bizarre behavior. They laughed as I helped Leslie out to the car. Had they seen her fall down in the parking lot, they would have thought it very funny.

For five months I was the friend that stuck closer than a brother. Then Leslie moved across the state and I did not see her again. She called me recently, at three in the morning, drinking again, and desperate. "I can't help you from so far away," I said. "Don't you have a friend there who can come and stay with you?"

"I have no one," she replied. "I'm so lonely."

She was right. She had no one. Her alcoholism had turned away everyone who tried to be friendly. Her many companions only enjoyed her when she was drinking with them.

In his book, *The Four Loves*, C. S. Lewis writes that true friendship has to be about something, "even if it were only an enthusiasm for dominoes or white mice." They must share a desire to see the same truth. "Those who have nothing can share nothing; those who are going nowhere can have no fellow-travelers." Leslie is going nowhere. Companions will go with her, to her eventual ruin. Until her life has direction, she will not have any friends.

Lord Jesus, thank you for my loyal friends who love me in spite of myself, and stick close to me in times of need. Thank you for your love which we share. Keep us from being exclusive. Make us open to new friendships, especially with those people with whom we can share the truth about you.

Is there someone at work or in church who wants to be your friend, but is too shy to take the first step? ☕

"It is not good to have zeal without knowledge, nor to be hasty and miss the way."

(Prov. 19:2)

A minister of a church in Manhattan had as a visitor in the morning worship service a young man who had recently arrived from Iowa. He was invited home for Sunday dinner where he was asked the inevitable question, "What are you doing here?" Without hesitation he replied that he had come to save New York City from its sins. The minister was glad to hear that, for he had the same objective. "How do you plan to do this?" he asked.

The young man answered that he had no plan. He was going to go out and talk about Jesus to everyone he met. Somehow he would find money for living expenses. Somehow he would find a place to stay. God would take care of it.

The minister had no doubt about God's ability to provide food and shelter. The fact that He often did it through a regular job was set aside for the moment. He had noted the young man's eagerness. He had already heard how he did, indeed, talk about Jesus to everyone he met: the owner of the corner deli; a Jewish tailor; three women who stood waiting for a bus.

Gently and lovingly he inquired as to the young evangelist's knowledge of the Scripture. Had he attended Bible school? The answer was, "No. I have only known the Lord for a year. But I want to save New York City!" Sadly, the minister acknowledged that very few people were similarly interested, but Manhattan was an exceedingly complex community, with thousands of religious groups. Their theologies were a challenge even to experienced ministers. The city was also noted for evil people who could easily exploit an Iowan who was not used to metropolitan culture.

He suggested that the young man take two years to ground himself in the Scriptures, and then return. He would be only twenty, with many years ahead to evangelize.

It was a hard decision, but he agreed. In time he did come back, ready to give an answer to everyone who asked him to give the reason for the hope that he had (1 Peter 4:15). Because of his knowledge and zeal, many came to know Christ.

Lord, I do not want to be zealous and ignorant. Nor do I want to be knowledgeable and apathetic. May I have enthusiasm for your work. Equip me with an understanding of your Word. Oh, Lord, guide me so I do not miss the way.

Is your church presently divided into two groups: those who want to get going on some project right away; and those who say, "Let's wait until we have more information"? Are you in one group or the other? How can you be a peacemaker? ☕

"Houses and wealth are inherited from parents, but a prudent wife is from the Lord."

(Prov. 19:14)

We don't hear much about prudence these days. This caution in regard to practical matters and provident care in the management of resources can also be termed "sensible," but that synonym lacks the force of thinking ahead, planning for the future.

A wife is prudent when she plans her menus for the week and shops accordingly. She is prudent when she uses one trip in the car to cover many stops. Prudence includes budgeting, investing, controlling credit, and not leaving all the lights on. It's knowing when eating out is a foolish expense, and when it's a necessary lift to depressed spirits.

This kind of wife is a gift from the Lord. She is very special, a person to be prized. A man can inherit his parents' house and furniture, but he can't get a wife that way. Families can do much for their grown-up sons, but they can't give them prudent wives.

Maybe you have been conscientiously doing your job every day, and wondering if it really matters. Housework has a demeaning ring to it. How can cleaning the toilet bowl compare with being a TV newscaster? Of what value is a homemade pizza? The family wolfs it down in six minutes flat anyway. Does everybody jump up from the table and yell, "Three cheers for mother!" They do not.

Take heart. You are of great value, a gift from the Lord. He put you in your present position to perform a managerial task that commands your keenest mental abilities. It involves much expertise, equally as much as running an office, or operating a restaurant.

You are a gift from the Lord.

Lord, sometimes I feel sorry for myself. This is self-pity, and not pleasing to you, nor good for me. Forgive me. Remind me through your Word that I do matter, that you do care. May I be prudent with the things you have entrusted to my care.

Feeling unappreciated? Read Psalm 8.

"He who is kind
to the poor
lends to the Lord,
and he will reward him
for what he has done."

(Prov. 19:17)

Those who think poverty can be eliminated with government programs are both unrealistic and unscriptural. "There will always be poor people in the land," says Deuteronomy 15:11. "The poor you will always have with you," said Jesus in Matthew 26:11.

While there are many things we can do to ease poverty, we cannot erase it. This does not mean we are to be calloused or indifferent. Repeatedly in Scripture, God's people are commanded to care for the poor. Under Mosaic law there was the seventh year when all debts were cancelled. In the other six years the Jews were to be openhanded and freely lending to anyone who had needs. Early in the establishment of the Christian church, there are reports of special offerings being taken to help the poor.

Because the poor are associated with ghettos in the inner city, they can become a remote social problem. If we don't live in the city, we find it hard to be kind. We may send a check to some agency offering relief, but we aren't being kind in the sense of personal involvement.

In every community there are the "invisible poor," going unnoticed because they do not live in groups. An elderly man staying alone in a small house at the end of the street is not eating properly, and his teeth need fixing. A divorcee is struggling to maintain the family home on her wages and child support. The family of an alcoholic is going into debt but not telling anyone. A Christian student is going without food so that she can get an education. To these poor, God calls us to be kind.

And what about the reward? Jesus talked about this, too, when He commended those who gave to the poor: "But when you give to the needy . . . your Father, who sees what is done in secret, will reward you" (Matt. 6:3). Later, in Matthew 25:46, we read of the reward—eternal life. This reward is not because we have earned it by our kindness to the poor or any other good works. It is the eternal life God gives to all who truly love Jesus Christ and have faith in Him. Kindness to the poor is merely one evidence of our faith.

Must I wait until I die to be rewarded? No, indeed! In this life we experience the joy of seeing others made happy. We receive the enrichment of their relationship with us. Our giving is the means whereby they hear and experience the gospel. We may be rewarded with seeing souls saved.

"He who is kind to the poor *lends* to the Lord." God always returns what He borrows.

Lord Jesus, because of you I am the child of a King, and rich beyond measure. Give me a generous spirit. Lead me to those silent poor who need my help.

Meditate on ten families in your neighborhood. Could one of them be poor? How would you know? ☕

"Discipline your son,
for in that
there is hope;
do not be
a willing party
to his death."

(Prov. 19:18)

Adonijah was a man who had never been disciplined. It was said of his father David, that "he had never interfered with him by asking, 'Why do you behave as you do?'" (1 Kings 1:6). Adonijah grew up with the idea that he could do whatever he pleased, even to being King of Israel. When this plan was thwarted, he took asylum on the horns of the altar in the tabernacle, and he was allowed to live if he showed himself to be a worthy man. Having had no experience in self-denial, he desired King Solomon's beautiful servant girl for his wife. For that request he was struck down, and he died.

Can a parent be a willing party to his child's death today? Certainly. Let him drive and drink liquor, and he will quite possibly kill himself and other people's children too. Let her date anybody she pleases and stay out all night, and she might be raped and stabbed. The toddler who doesn't learn "no" will run in front of a car, or drink poison. The son who endlessly indulges in fatty foods will develop an obesity problem that taxes his heart to the limit.

The proverb does not say there is hope in *punishment*. Discipline means teaching, guidance, and encouragement. It is derived from the biblical word "disciple"—one who follows the teachings of a leader. The immediate goal is to make your children disciples. The long-term goal is the development of compliant wills open to the claims of Christ. The son who accepts these has the hope of eternal life.

Oh Father, I do not want my children to die. Help me to discipline them according to your Word. May I be used to lead them to Jesus Christ, their Savior.

Do not assume that your children are Christians just because they are your children. Take time to explain salvation to each one. Pray for their understanding and acceptance.

> ## "Listen to advice and accept instruction, and in the end you will become wise."
>
> (Prov. 19:20)

It all depends, of course, on the kind of advice you're listening to. For every magazine and book telling us to do something one way, there is another magazine or book promoting an opposite view. A diet which forbids desserts is followed by one based upon a slice of apple pie every day. One friend advises us to go into nursing. Another suggests selling fork lifts. When we turn to the Bible, we find no specific information on either weight loss or employment counseling.

Because we are sinners, we can't take a bit of data and base our decision on it alone. We must take that information and view it in the total context of God's Word. Whether or not we buy something in a store, for example, depends upon stewardship principles in Scripture. Those principles become an intrinsic part of our nature as we yield ourselves to the Holy Spirit, the teacher Christ has given us. To know the Holy Spirit, we must know Christ as our Lord and Savior.

Wisdom begins, then, with a relationship with Christ. This relationship determines our world-and-life view. Christ calls us to obedience to the Scriptures. "If you love me, you will obey what I command," He says in John 14:25.

For Christmas last year, we were given a fifteen-hundred-piece jigsaw puzzle. First we assembled the frame, and then the colored section—a relatively easy task. We were left with about three hundred black pieces. It took eight people two months to put that puzzle together. We had to depend on shape, so we organized the pieces according to four general configurations. Then someone discovered that the entire puzzle was a repeat of patterns. By taking the shapes, and repeating the patterns, the final stage was a breeze. After we had it all together we glued it and hung it on the wall.

The Christian life is like a puzzle. The frame is our belonging to Christ. The colored pieces are those obvious commandments too clear to be missed. (The Ten Commandments might be considered the red pieces.) The black pieces are those decisions not directly spoken of. Should I buy a ranch house or a condominium? Where can I serve God best? We view these in their relation to the frame and the colored pieces. Just like putting together that fifteen-hundred-piece puzzle, we use the help of other people—Christian counselors and friends that God has given us. He doesn't expect us to assemble our jigsaw puzzle life alone.

This is becoming wise: Jesus as the framework, Scripture as the base, and Christian counsel for the difficult decisions.

Dear God. I confess that I do not always want to be wise. I am too often satisfied with ignorance. Forgive me. Make me sensitive to the leading of your Spirit. Teach me through your Word. Give me an accepting heart.

Wisdom is a long-term investment. ☕

"He who robs his father
and drives out his mother
is a son who brings
shame and disgrace."

(Prov. 19:26)

Robbery carries with it a picture of a masked thief, breaking into a house, scooping up the family silver, and dropping it into a sack. We think of bank robbers with nylon stockings over their faces or two bandits holding up a stage coach. None of these examples quite fits the idea of robbing one's father.

When viewed in the general context of taking what belongs to someone else, we see robbery of parents as a common practice. There is the son who borrows his father's car and doesn't fill the gas tank, and the daughter who takes a job and expects Mom to baby-sit all day. Children can rob elderly parents of their dignity and self-value by subtly treating them as mindless creatures. Children can also rob middle-aged parents of their independence by demanding all the attention and favors they had when they were young.

There comes a time in the teen-age years when sons and daughters see themselves as full-fledged adults with marvelous capabilities. Youthful egos reach unprecedented heights. Poor old Dad and Mom are viewed as a hopelessly out-dated couple, muddling through without the wisdom of modern high schools and television programs. When these sons and daughters reach their twenties this view often changes. The moment of crisis comes when the dinner guests are to arrive in fifteen minutes, and only a phone call to Mother will explain how to get the gelatine salad to fall perfectly into the circle of lettuce leaves. Or it may be father's tour of the proposed new home which points up its poor construction.

Some children never come to that place where they recognize their parents as knowledgeable persons. They may express their disdain with open rebellion, ridicule, or masked tolerance. They may ignore their parents all together, with no more communication other than a yearly Christmas card. In such cases they have robbed their fathers and mothers of their rightful roles as parents. They have literally driven them out of their lives.

God's Word condemns this dehumanization, and calls those who practice it a shame and disgrace.

Oh, Lord, am I guilty of dehumanizing my parents? Have I robbed them of their right to parent me, even as old as I am? Forgive me. Help me to love my father and mother so much that they will regard me as a blessing.

This day, no matter how busy you are, do something kind for your parents, no matter where they are. ☕

"Wine is a mocker and beer a brawler; whoever is led astray by them is not wise."

(Prov. 20:1)

Why is liquor a mocker? It lets us think we won't become victims of it.

Why is liquor a brawler? It leads to aggressive behavior.

Since liquor is so bad for us, we would expect the Scripture to say so forthrightly. The fact that it does not, gives many people the needed justification for drinking it, which they were going to do anyway. "Aha", they say, "Jesus turned water into wine at the wedding. Paul said a little wine is good for the stomach. If *they* thought liquor was all right, there can't be anything wrong with it."

Just a minute. Judean wine was not Scotch whiskey. That high-ball you have pictured in the magazine ad is not like the watered-down beverage common in first-century Jewish diets. Their wine did not have as great an ability to intoxicate. Furthermore, drinking it in the controlled situations mentioned in the Bible was far different from stopping in a bar after work and "having a few with the girls." Wine was a beverage accompanying food. It was not touted as a means to be popular, self-important, or sexy. Early Christians didn't sit in their houses and see TV programs in which liquor was used to ease every anxious situation. Wine was essentially used to ease thirst.

It is estimated that one out of every ten women in the United States is an alcoholic. Liquor has led those women astray, clamping them into a grip that nothing short of total abstinence can release. Help for them requires professional counsel, even in the context of commitment to Christ.

To those nine out of ten women who are not alcoholics, note this verse which points out that liquor can lead you astray. At this point in your life it may not seem to be such a serious matter to drink wine or beer. You may even be considering it for the first time. Your parents were opposed to liquor, so you never tried it. Now you are on your own, and you find it tempting.

Liquor and those who drink it can make a fool out of you. Can you "handle" just one drink? You do not know. Are you a potential alcoholic? You do not know. Will your drinking encourage someone else? Almost assuredly. Will she be able to handle it? Is she a potential alcoholic? Again, you do not know. Wisdom, says this proverb, is maintaining your present direction. Continue to abstain.

Everybody drinks but me, Lord. Give me the courage to be different. Give me the strength to encourage others not to drink, either.

Do you know an alcoholic? Pray for her. Urge her to seek Christian counsel. ☕

"Many a man claims to have unfailing love, but a faithful man who can find?"

(Prov. 20:6)

This is a time when relationships are receiving much attention in the church. Caring and sharing is a theme running through small groups, prayer meetings, and Bible studies. The coldness and impersonalness that was characteristic of some churches is being broken down. Praise God! Paul says, "Each of you should look not only to your own interests, but also to the interests of others" (Phil. 2:4). We are to go beyond the "Hello, how are you?"—"Fine, how are you?" verbal exchange, to a sincere concern.

The woman who takes Paul's admonition seriously, soon finds that she cannot be an intimate friend to everyone. She cannot meet the needs of every person who walks through the church door. Being a faithful friend, one who is available at any time for sacrificial service, has certain definite limitations of time and energy.

What do we do to solve the problem? We begin by praying daily that the Lord will direct us to the friendships of His choosing. This may put us in contact with other women we would not choose otherwise. Last summer, when I earnestly prayed for a new friend in my own neighborhood, I, who do not like dogs, was led to a woman who owns seven!

When we have placed the matter in the Lord's hands, we no longer need to feel anxious about all those people we cannot help. Our place is to pray that they will find faithful friends. We may have an active part in this, introducing two people of similar interests, or having a group of women over for morning coffee and letting friends find each other.

We may be led by the Lord to change our own life-style so that we can practice unfailing love. This can take the form of simpler cooking and housekeeping, so that we are more available, or cutting back on the entanglements of clubs and related projects so we are free to perform deeds of mercy. The faithful person called for in this proverb is not much good if she can't be found.

Thank you, Lord, for my faithful friends. They have shown unfailing love to me, and I am grateful. Lead me, today, to those whom you would have me help. May I be content with your choice.

Invite over for a simple lunch two women who could help each other.

"Even a child is
known by his actions,
by whether his conduct
is pure and right."

(Prov. 20:11)

Some psychologists believe a child's character is formed by the time he is four. Others say by ten. Whatever the age, the time to influence children is brief. By junior high, most American children have reached a stage of hardness and sophistication that makes character building almost impossible.

How is character formed? Few dispute the belief that

the young learn by modeling the old. The father who boasts at the dinner table how he got his traffic ticket fixed is teaching deceit, no matter how much he talks about honesty as a virtue. The mother who sends a casserole to every sick family in the neighborhood is teaching compassion, even though she may never make it a subject of conversation.

Pure and right conduct is marred at times by sin. How we handle our sin is the concrete block upon which all other character is built. Do we repent sincerely? Can we admit our failure to others? Do we make restitution where it is possible? Can we then let the matter rest, and go on with positive feelings and actions?

Our response when we are sinned against is likewise a behavior carefully observed by children. Can we truly forgive, and *forget?* Can we learn to love that person? As we apply Biblical principles within and without the home, we are modeling conduct which is readily observable and possible to emulate. Parents who are open in their struggle with sin encourage their children to put up the same fight.

It is easy to lose the awesome responsibility of parenthood once the first baby is into its pre-school years. Mother and father develop an arrogance often expressed in, "Do as I say and not what I do." The "even" in this proverb serves to remind us that a mother is known by her actions, too.

Parenting is hard work, Lord. I make mistakes. Guide me. Give me a humble spirit. Help me to be honest with myself and with my children. And Lord, guide them. Help them to be honest with themselves and with me.

Whatever else you do today, pray with each of your children. ☕

"'It's no good,
it's no good!'
says the buyer;
then off he goes
and boasts about
his purchase."

(Prov. 20:14)

Why is there more traffic on our street on Wednesday than any other day? On Wednesdays the free newspaper is delivered. It contains notices of all the garage sales. One-family, six-family, neighborhood, and senior-high-school-band-parents garage sales! You can buy a vase from the nickle and dime table. You may find an antique. Our minister's wife paid two dollars for a musical tea pot.

Operating a garage sale requires a shrewd sense of business. Knowing how to display merchandise properly increases sales. Knowing what to charge and when to haggle takes experience. How long should you hold out on that kitchen table? It's worth more than you've been offered, but you don't want to store it in the basement for another year. Your husband may change his mind about that set of golf clubs if you don't get rid of them today. What should you do?

Shopping at garage sales takes expertise, too. Amid all the junk there may be a real treasure—something definitely under-priced. Part of the game is showing off to your friends. Six ceramic flower pots and a macramé plant holder for five dollars! How about that?

Surely, the Lord has more important things to do than care about garage sales. And yet, here is a little gem of a verse for the Wednesday shoppers. Because buying and selling constitutes an important point of contact for individuals, it is imperative that we deal honestly. Our witness for Christ is at stake, even as we look through a rack of used dresses. We dare not take advantage of the seller's ignorance. When tragic circumstances, such as a divorce, have forced the seller to earn extra money, or move away, we have a serious responsibility to pay a fair price.

Can you imagine what would happen if we went to a garage sale, found something we really needed, and told the seller we wanted to pay more than she was asking? She'd certainly want to know what made us do something so unusual. Wouldn't it be great to tell her?

Lord, help me to remember that in my buying and selling, I represent you. Make me honest. Give me opportunities, even at garage sales, to witness in your name. Thank you.

As an expression of love, give something away today. ☕

"Make plans
by seeking advice;
if you wage war,
obtain guidance."

(Prov. 20:18)

The Hebrew word for guidance in this verse refers to the rigging of a ship. The counsel we seek is to be used for handling and steering our situation. We take into account all the various factors which can influence our decision, and make our judgments on the basis of the means we have at hand.

It is not uncommon for Christians to seek help with their problems. But here we are told to seek advice when we make plans. Where shall we spend our vacation? What size family is best for us? When shall I finish college? Even such a practical matter as how to redecorate the kitchen can turn out better with the advice of a friend. Edith may suggest a sky light to make the room much brighter. We hadn't thought of that.

Within the church fellowship are many resource people. The church officers, called by God to oversee His work, have wisdom and experience. Many in the church have jobs and education which give them the expertise we need, with the additional value of a Christian perspective. Realtors, investment brokers, and bankers, can advise on financial matters. Mechanics know about cars. Teachers can help with the problems arising when the children are in school. Often this advice is free. When it is regularly given for a price, we should be glad to pay.

The prayer meeting, at which needs are shared and brought before God for His direction, is a powerful source of help that many people never use. A man who lost his job and planned to move out of his house, brought the matter before his prayer group. Through their prayers and subsequent counsel, he found a new job without relocating. A woman suffering with arthritis planned to undergo radical therapy until she was led to an out-of-state doctor whose treatment gave her much relief.

It is not God's intention that we plan on our own. Over and over again He reminds us in Scripture that we are part of a body. "... its parts should have equal concern for each other" (1 Cor. 12:25). Within this body we should seek advice.

Dear Lord, I don't know everything. I need advice. Make me willing to seek it and accept it. Burden me to pray with others, that all of us may know the blessings of Your counsel.

What kind of wars can we wage today? Against inflation, over-weight, heresy, and pornography. How many others can you name? ☕

"Do not say, 'I'll pay you back for this wrong!' Wait for the Lord, and he will deliver you."

(Prov. 20:22)

Sweet is revenge, especially to women," said Lord Byron. To the unregenerate heart there is nothing more satisfying than getting back at someone. But to those who belong to Jesus Christ, revenge has absolutely no place. When we have been wronged, we are to let God carry out justice in whatever way He sees fit. The bolt of lightening we might wish for will probably not occur. God's method may test our patience to the limit. We are to wait for Him to act.

This waiting is not to be a passive, but seething, hatred in our hearts. We are not to hope our offender suffers a terrible calamity, that she "gets what's coming to her." This attitude would not distinguish us from much of the world. Jesus calls His followers to a positive, active response. "Love your enemies and pray for those who persecute you," He says (Matt. 5:44). "Really, Lord?" we respond. "Isn't that asking a lot, after all she's done to me?"

Jesus always asks a lot. But when He asks, He enables. He has left us His Spirit to give us power, love, and self-discipline (2 Tim. 1:7). We have Jesus' example, as He forgave those who nailed him to the cross. If anyone had justification for revenge, it was Jesus, and yet He forgave. Indeed, we have done wrong and deserved God's revenge, and we have been forgiven.

But Jesus asks for more than a loving feeling. We are to love by our actions—caring for our enemies—actually giving them food and water (Rom. 12:20). Somebody lies about me at work, so I take her a loaf of home-baked wheat bread? Yes. My neighbor backs into my new car, and I invite her in for a glass of ice tea? Yes.

Jesus gives us further enablement—a worthy goal. Our ultimate desire is that our enemy be won to Christ. This is the reward we want for our kindness. This is the Lord's supreme deliverance for the avenged.

Oh Lord, you are expecting me to do some very hard things. I would like to enjoy my hateful, revengeful feelings. Take them from me. Cleanse me so that I can love my enemies. It's not going to be easy.

Is there someone you would like to pay back for a wrong? What can you do today to show love? ☕

> ## "All a man's ways seem right to him, but the Lord weighs the heart."
>
> (Prov. 21:2)

When Will came home with the news that he had been promoted to vice-president, Barbara's first thought was Oyster Bay. She didn't say it out loud, of course, but with Will's increase in salary they could afford to move to a bigger house. Not that Osprey Park wasn't nice. They had lived there for ten years. Will had put in a fabulous vegetable garden, screened in the patio, and even remodeled the kitchen. But Oyster Bay had class.

Will wouldn't want to move. He liked being settled. Barbara decided not to say anything right now. She would pray about the matter—ask the Lord for a sign.

A week later Doris Brewer called from Palms Realty. "Barbara, you told me a year ago how much you wanted to move to Oyster Bay. I just got word that there's a house on the outer circle. Would you like to give it a look before everyone else does?" The Lord had given Barbara her first sign.

The house was beautiful. Four large bedrooms, patio with pool, even a boat dock. The children would love it. But how could she convince Will? Barbara prayed again, "Lord, prepare his heart."

That night after dinner, Barbara asked Will how his mother was doing. "Not too well. She tires so easily. She seems forgetful. She ought to move out of that house."

"Will, why don't we offer to take care of her? I know I could manage."

"In this house? There aren't enough bedrooms. You

136

remember how miserable we were when she shared with Kitty two years ago? You can't put a seventy-year-old woman and a junior-high student in the same room."

"We could move to a bigger house. There's a lovely home for sale on Oyster Bay. I looked at it today. It has four bedrooms. One is perfect for your mother."

Will agreed to think about it. Barbara presented all the other arguments—how good it would be for the children, the extra space for vice-presidential entertaining, and the fun of having their own boat. But really, the main reason to move was to care for Will's mother.

Two weeks later they signed the papers. They sold the house in Osprey Park. Will was strangely quiet the day the van came. He spent the day out in the garden, of all things, picking the last tomatoes. The children found it hard to say goodby to old friends.

Barbara's days were filled with redecorating and buying new furniture. Will asked about moving his mother but Barbara had to put the matter off. "You can't put an old woman in a house that's all torn up by painters and paperers. Just as soon as they're gone, we'll move her in."

About three months elapsed before the way was clear. By then Will's mother was too sick to move. The doctor at the geriatric center gave her a few weeks to live, at the most. When she died, Barbara was really sad. But the old woman would have been terribly hard to care for. And they did have a lovely guest room now, so something good had come out of the situation. Barbara would thank the Lord for working things out the way He did.

Lord, I can easily fool myself into doing what I want to. Teach me your will through your Word. Make me honest with myself.

Do you use Christian principles to manipulate people? How about motives? See Proverbs 16:2. ☕

"He who loves pleasure
will become poor;
whoever loves wine and oil
will never become rich."

(Prov. 21:17)

Just as I suspected—Christians aren't supposed to have any fun.

No, that's not the point here. The word "pleasure" is the same word used for "joy." This joy, or pleasure, or feeling of happiness, is to be the *result* of our activity, not the object. We may set as our goal for the day the completion of a particular office task, and when it is done, feel a beautiful sense of satisfaction that is truly pleasurable. We may set as our goal for the day watching ten hours of television, and end up being bored, tired, and not happy at all.

There is, of course, a pragmatic result of pleasure-loving. It pays no income. Wine and oil are symbols of indulgence in lavish entertainment; in our day we might say champagne and caviar. The person who spends her time loving them can become poor by eating and drinking to the point where she cannot work, or spending so much money on them that she has nothing left for essentials. There are "bums" on Skid Row who lie in the streets as highly visible reminders of what alcohol can do. Less obvious are those women at home who love their credit cards and use them to charge all kinds of pleasure, from shopping to expensive lunches.

I heard, recently, of a famous wealthy family that owed so much money to the townspeople that they couldn't return home to live in their Venetian-style mansion on the Gulf of Mexico. When the parents died, there was no money left for the children to inherit. The mansion became part of a state park.

Work can be pleasurable. So can prayer. Doing something for someone else can actually make the soul laugh. When our object is to please God, joy is a natural result. This feeling of happiness can actually make us more attractive to hire and more desirable to keep in the job.

Dear God, help me to get my goals straight. Give me useful work to do, loving relationships, opportunities to help others, surprises in the world around me. I await, with confidence, the joy these will bring.

Is there a "wine and oil" which takes too much of your money? Ask others to pray for you. 🍵

"There is no wisdom,
no insight, no plan
that can succeed
against the Lord."

(Prov. 21:30)

Haman found this thought to be true. He had a clever plan to get rid of Mordecai, who would not kneel down and pay him honor. When he learned that Mordecai was a Jew, he devised a plan to exterminate all the other Jews, too. But God had made Esther the queen for just such a time as this. Through her appeal to King Xerxes, the Jews were saved. The deceitful Haman was hanged on the very gallows he had prepared for Esther's Uncle Mordecai.

Within the church today there are people making plans as if God wouldn't notice. When an important issue is announced for a congregational meeting, all the members who rarely come to church are rallied to vote for one side or the other. A committee chairman is voted out of office while she's away on vacation. A wealthy woman waits to make a huge donation to the building fund at the last minute and then uses her popularity to influence the design of the new sanctuary.

Because such manipulations seem to work, we may think that God is fooled. But the bitterness that results causes strife and division within the church. God may choose to let natural reactions take their course, or He may intervene directly, but such plans do not ultimately succeed. There is a figurative hanging somewhere down the road.

In Isaiah 29:14 the Lord says of those people who honor Him with their lips but not their hearts: "the wisdom of the wise will perish, the intelligence of the intelligent will vanish." When we make plans, God expects to be consulted. The wisdom He gives us will bring success.

I think I know what is the best thing to do, Lord. Show me in your Word if I am right. Help me to assess my circumstances correctly. Humble me to stop if I am wrong.

Are there divisions in your church? Read 1 Corinthians 3.

"The horse is made ready for the day of battle, but victory rests with the Lord."

(Prov. 21:31)

This is a proverb about war. A related passage is found in Psalm 20:7—"Some trust in chariots and some in horses, but we trust in the name of the Lord our God." That was written by David, who was a soldier. From the day when he faced Goliath as a young man, to the day in his old age when he faced the sword of the Lord's angel, David was involved in battle.

We should note that the Scripture doesn't condemn horses and chariots. It doesn't say we are to fight without weapons. Certainly, when we are called into battle we are to go equipped and trained. But we are not to trust in our weapons nor credit them with the victory. That is the

Lord's doing. To Him goes all the credit for our success.

Most of us will never see an actual battlefield. Even if women are registered for the draft, and even if our nation is forced to fight another nation, most women will be in non-combative situations. We do have wars to fight, however. There is the constant battle with Satan. Paul tells us the armor we need for that in Ephesians 6. There are times when we have to fight heresy within the church. For this we need to be equipped with the truth of God. We may have to fight for morality, and stand up at the next parent-teacher meeting and protest the proposed curriculum in sex education.

Or the battle may not be religious at all. Our fight can be to preserve the character of our neighborhood against further commercialization, or for better law enforcement. Parents of retarded children have fought for better schools and sheltered workshops.

For these kinds of battles our horses and chariots are facts and proper communication. We are obligated to learn all we can about the situation, and know how to present it so we get results. Both the church and the world have their systems for getting things changed. As Christians, we must understand them and use them.

Our verbal horses are only the tools of victory. How we approach the enemy, the attitude in our hearts, the strategy for winning, all depend upon the leading of the Lord. It is to Him that we look for strength and wisdom. The praise for victory goes only to Him.

I confess that I'm not much of a fighter, Lord. I don't like taking a stand against evil. Show me when I am supposed to be a soldier. Give me courage and skill. May I trust in you to bring me victory and peace.

Is God powerful enough to win a fight? Read Psalm 66.

Jean Andreno,

"A good name is more desirable
than great riches;
to be esteemed is better
than silver or gold."

(Prov. 22:1)

I approached my first day in Spanish 1 with fear and palpitations. My teacher would be Mrs. Cusano—terror of the language department—who believed that high school sophomores should come to class prepared and eager, every day of the year. Those who did not, suffered her wrath. My brother had taken French with Mrs. Cusano nine years ago, and he still remembered her verbal whipping when he was not alert. If my good-natured, mannerly brother had suffered, what chance did I have?

I entered the classroom as quietly as the others, and

slipped into a middle seat. Mrs. Cusano proceeded to take roll, coming to each desk and asking us to write our names on a paper that took form, in our imaginations, as a list of prisoners ready for execution. She stopped beside me and waited while I wrote "Jean Andreae." Picking the paper up, she read it carefully and then asked, "Are you Marcus Andreae's sister?" "Yes," I replied with trembling lips. "Well, then, you sit right up here." and she pointed to the first desk in my row.

Nine years, and she had not forgotten! I spent the entire year directly beneath her withering gaze, all because of my brother and his occasional failings in French. Oh, the power of a name! Had I been the richest student in Wilbur H. Lynch High School, it would not have made the slightest difference to Mrs. Cusano.

What is my name? It's my character, my reputation. It's all that I am. To be regarded with love and respect means more than silver and gold, even at today's prices.

In John 14:22 a man named Judas asks Jesus a very thoughtful question. He was one of the twelve apostles, also called Thaddeus, the son or perhaps the brother of James, and evidently a good man. John carefully distinguishes him from that other Judas, the betrayer of Christ. How hard it must have been for the good Judas! Everywhere he went, he had to explain, "No, I'm not Judas Iscariot." Even today, the name Judas is despised.

Lord, I find myself desiring great riches. It would be wonderful to have all the bills paid. Stop me from getting money in a dishonorable way that will damage my reputation. Show me the value of good character.

Think of all the times you sign your name—checks, contracts, letters, service orders, credit cards, etc. Reflect on what your signature means. ☕

"Train a child in
the way he should go,
and when he is old
he will not turn from it."

(Prov. 22:6)

A sixth-grade teacher has a pupil who is regularly seeing a psychiatrist for anxiety and tension. She knew the boy was in trouble the day he cried over his report card. He had all A's except for one B, and he knew that when his father saw that one B, he was going to be furious. The boy's father is an ophthalmologist, and his grandfather is an ophthalmologist. Therefore, the boy also plans to be an ophthalmologist. How will he ever get into medical school with a B in sixth-grade language arts?

Some parents treat their children like Jello. Pick out a nicely shaped mold, pour the child into it, and when she sets, she'll be perfect. The problem begins when the parents pick out the mold. They try to make a star-shaped boy into a fish, or a 9 x 13 pan girl into a fluted, three-tiered, jeweled masterpiece.

We can paraphrase this proverb and get its true meaning. "Train up a child according to his way, and when he is old he will not depart from it"—not according to his father's way, nor his mother's way, but *his* way. His individuality and vocation are to be respected. As parents we have the responsibility to choose our child's food, clothing, and vaccinations, but beyond these basic decisions, there is much room for the child to make choices of his own.

Neither this proverb, nor any other passage in Scripture, implies that parents are to neglect spiritual instruction. The home is the best school for this. Bible stories, catechism, and prayer are most effective in the hands of the child's best teachers—his parents. But it is as Christian models that parents teach their children the most. Children learn best not by their parents pretending perfection, but by their openly relying on God to work changes in their lives.

A man of thirty remarked that the greatest evidence of the Holy Spirit he had seen was the way He took away his father's violent temper. For many years the son and his father had prayed about it together, and the son had watched God work the change in his father's life.

I am sorry for the times I have pushed my children into a mold that was neither theirs nor yours, Lord. Help me to see them as individuals, each in your image and unique. Keep me steadfast in teaching them your Word, when there are so many other activities going on.

If you have never prayed with your children, make a beginning today. Share with them one problem in your life and ask their help.

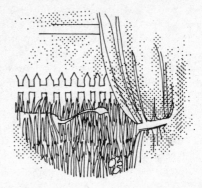

"The sluggard says,
'There is a lion outside!'
or 'I will be murdered
in the streets!' "

(Prov. 22:13)

A sluggard would be comical if she weren't so tragic. She doesn't know she is lazy. After all, there may be a lion outside. True, the possibility is unlikely, unless there has been an escape at the zoo, but she can't be sure. Better put off mowing the grass.

Sluggards rarely start anything, and they even more rarely finish anything. They live in a world of "going to": "I am going to remodel my kitchen"; "I am going to fly to Seattle to visit my sick father." If the trip keeps getting delayed, father dies before a relationship is restored.

How does a person become "unsluggarded"? First, by acknowledging the problem. Unfortunately, sluggards think their problem is really a virtue. They don't think they're lazy, just cautious, or conserving their energy, or waiting for a better time. Sluggards need prodders to expose their rationalizations and get them moving.

Prodders can be friends—the wonderful kind that are honest but supportive. A Bible passage, a sermon, even part of a sermon, can prod us to self-examination. We may find that we are not sluggards, that our excuses are valid. It is possible for people to be murdered in the streets these days. We are wise not to walk alone at night.

If we suspect that sluggardness is a problem, we can ask for help. God may answer through a friend, or His Word, or a means we can't foresee, but He will answer. It is His desire that we use the energy and talent that we have. In Isaiah 41:29 is the promise: He gives strength to the weary and increases the power of the weak.

We can be assured that God knows the difference between weakness and weariness. There are times when we are too exhausted to do one more thing than fall into bed. God understands. His Son became weary too. Whether our problem is a long-range condition, or a temporary distress, we can call upon God for strength.

Lord, I don't see myself the way you do. I may be a sluggard and not have the slightest idea. Show me through your Word that I have valid reasons for not doing something, or that I am just making excuses. Help me to get going on the work that you want me to do.

Rather than overwhelm yourself with a list of twenty-four jobs that you mean to get done this year, pick two for each month, and ask someone to check on you for those two.

"Do you see a man
skilled in his work?
He will serve before kings;
he will not serve
before obscure men."

(Prov. 22:39)

I have known many skilled workers who have never served before kings. With the shortage of kings in the world today, and the abundance of "do-it-yourselfers," that's understandable. A king can use just so many bookshelves and stereo cabinets.

A modern paraphrase might be: He will have a good job with a profitable company; what he does will be noticed. The point is that a skilled worker puts workmanship before prospects. He gets a new car in perfect running order before he finds a buyer. She updates her real estate knowledge even though no one is looking for a house. The skilled worker who wants to please God is thorough and accurate regardless of who will be checking.

Skilled work is so rare today that we don't expect it. We know our new car will have ten things wrong with it. We know we'll have to resew the buttons on our new coat. It was *after* I had my typewriter repaired that the roller knob fell off. A friend said, "If that's all that went wrong you should be happy." I am not happy with a left-handed typewriter, exclusive an object though it may be.

Why does God care about shoddiness? He cares about honesty, first of all. We should deserve our wages. The customer should get what she pays for. He also is concerned about dependability. A poor piece of work causes someone else irritation, loss of time, perhaps even harm. God also cares about beauty. A neatly kept ledger has a form and design that testifies to the care of the bookkeeper. The surgeon who describes an operation as a "beautiful piece of work," is speaking quite properly. By her work the Christian reflects her creator, who has made all things perfectly.

Father, I confess that sometimes I just throw things together. (I'm too embarrassed to wear that skirt I made.) I get tired, or don't leave enough time, or don't read the directions. Sometimes I just don't care. Help me work carefully, and do my best, so that You will be glorified.

A Song of Work: Read Psalm 19.

"Do not wear yourself out
to get rich;
have the wisdom
to show restraint."

(Prov. 23:4)

With more women employed outside the home, more women are getting heart attacks, more women are getting ulcers, more women are smoking, and more women are getting lung cancer. Stress of the business world is not the only cause. Women with families are still doing most of the housekeeping they did when they weren't employed.

So, after nine hours to, from, and on the job, they still must cook, clean, shop, do laundry, and go to school conferences. Saturday means putting twenty hours of chores into ten.

What is the reason for all this frenetic activity? It is basically economic necessity, although fulfillment has something to do with it. It now takes two incomes to do what one used to do. In an increasing number of one-parent households, the mother receives no alimony; her job is a matter of survival.

The Bible is not against women being employed. No condemnation is given to Lydia, described in Acts 16; and the exemplary working wife in Proverbs 31 is praised. Scripture does speak against work when it is motivated by greed, when the job becomes all-important, filling up days and nights well beyond the normal work load.

Restraint applies not only to hours on the job, but also to the desire for things. God recognizes the difference between groceries or shoes, and wanting a third television set. To resist the subtle pressures of a higher standard of living takes wisdom. Again, we are led to study God's Word and seek counsel from other Christians. Left to our own desires, we can propel ourselves into a state of sickness which may not have a cure.

Yes, Father, there have been many times when I was worn out. You graciously refreshed me and gave me strength. Help me not to presume upon your grace. Curb my desire for luxuries. Let me work only for what is really necessary.

How many hours of your week are involved with your job, either in or out of the home? Do you have time to be alone with God? Attend church? Relax with others in the family? Relax with yourself? Read Proverbs 23:5 and 1 Timothy 6:6–10. 🍵

> "Do not withhold
> discipline from a child;
> if you punish him with a rod,
> he will not die."
>
> (Prov. 23:13)

I have yet to meet a parent who didn't spank his child at least once for spilling his milk. Anger at the inept table manners of pre-schoolers seems to be a universal problem.

There is a definite difference between misbehavior because of emotional or physical limitations, and willful disobedience. The child who cries uncontrollably after a day of sitting in a stroller while mother shops, is not naughty. She's exhausted. The child who is told not to eat anything before supper, and then takes four chocolate chip cookies, is disobeying and needs to be punished. In spite of his howling, he will not die from a brief and direct spanking. On the contrary, respect for authority will prolong his life.

Discipline implies proper conduct on the part of the parent as well as the child. A disciplined parent does not indulge her own passions, striking out because she herself is frustrated, fatigued, or angry at someone else who is unavailable. Marital disagreements have a way of venting themselves on the helpless children. "You're just like your father!"

We are not to withhold punishment when it is warranted. Our actions should be immediate, brief, and then forgotten. Constant harping back to the problem initiates deep rebellion. Threatening is a disaster which brings on emotional turmoil as each party stretches his own will to the limit. Parents who threaten soon lose all credibility. Children learn to manipulate them to their own advantage.

Destructive punishment is not taught in Scripture, but discipline is quite biblical. Hebrews 12:11 says that "No discipline seems pleasant at the time, but painful. Later on, however, it produces a harvest of righteousness and peace for those who have been trained by it."

I want my family to have righteousness and peace, Lord. Screaming and arguing, irresponsibility, and disregard for others make us miserable. Give me the wisdom to discipline my children so that each one will reflect the character of your Son.

Parents need discipline too. Read Hebrews 12. 🍵

"Who has woe?
Who has sorrow?
Those who linger over wine,
who go to sample
bowls of mixed wine."

(Prov. 23:29–30)

The woman who is lingering and sampling is not your casual drinker. She is a drunk.

A few years ago we welcomed into our home a woman from the psychiatric floor of a nearby hospital. She was described as depressed and in need of temporary care until she found a job and her own apartment. A month after she moved in she admitted that she "had a problem with alcohol." In the months that followed that, as we coped with her hysteria, hallucinations, mysterious absences, automobile accidents, blackouts, and stupors, we learned to call her condition what it was—alcoholism. She was a drunk.

What woe and sorrow she had! Because of her love for wine (she would drink a whole bottle of Cold Duck and attempt suicide), she lost her husband, three children, home, and furniture. When her divorce was finally settled, all her possessions, representing twenty years of work, fit into a concrete storage locker. Today she lives across the state, changing jobs when her alcoholism is discovered. Her family has disowned her. She has no friends.

In Isaiah 5:11 we read, "Woe to those who rise early in the morning to run after their drinks, who stay up late at night till they are inflamed with wine." That's alcoholism. Is there any hope? Yes, through the power of the Holy Spirit, a life indwelt by Him, through commitment to Jesus Christ, can overcome the magnetic force of liquor. But alcoholics often do not want help until life has become so unbearable that there is no way out.

As we studied alcoholism, for our survival as much as to help our guest, we learned that making excuses for it, and covering it up, are the worst possible ways to handle it. All authorities agree that the alcoholic must be allowed to suffer, to feel the consequences of her drinking, even if it means utter degradation. It is very hard for her family to allow this to happen. For the compassionate Christian, it is literally painful. But it must occur.

Do you have an alcoholic in your home? Stop enduring and get help.

Dear God, I pray today for all those women who are alcoholics. How miserable they are. How sad. By your grace, save their souls. Empower them by your Holy Spirit to stop drinking. Lead their families to admit openly their own suffering.

Exposing an alcoholic in the family begins a year of terrible anguish. But can it be any worse than the humiliation and misery of the effects of drunkenness? Is it not better to endure anguish so that the victim can be helped? 🍵

"Do not envy wicked men, do not desire their company."

(Prov. 24:1)

First we're told to get out of our little Christian orbits and penetrate worldly outer space. Now we're told to avoid bad company. How can we witness to the unsaved if we don't know any? It seems to me that I must sincerely want to be with unbelievers if my witness is to have any credibility at all.

First, we must be sure of our motives. Do we socialize with the unsaved because we like their life-style? Do we wish we could have the possessions they have, and the freedom to use them? I can't justify eating in expensive restaurants, but if I pal around with rich women, I have to eat where they do. (It's only courteous, you understand, and sometimes they pay for it.) I really shouldn't be spending a whole evening seeing an "R" movie, but if I go with an unsaved friend, I may have an opportunity to use the film as a launching pad into the gospel. (Well, yes, I sort of want to see the movie anyway.) Are we being truthful?

Second, we must be sure of our desires. "Company" here implies a comradeship, a wanting them to like us. We make the accommodation, shaving off a little moral standard here, a chunk of spiritual responsibility there, so we won't be too offensive. We desire their company, we really want it very much. We accommodate, this time using Paul's oft-quoted direction to be all things to all men, omitting the fact that Paul never knowingly sinned to become so.

Christ kept company with wicked men, not out of envy, but out of pity. He saw the wretchedness of the unsaved. "When he saw the crowds, he had compassion on them, because they were harassed and helpless, like sheep without a shepherd" (Matt. 9:50). He ate with sinners so they might repent of their sins. His motive was always to reach the lost. Praise God for those humble servants who are willing to live with the most vile of people in order to witness for the Savior.

Father, I pray today for Christians working in prisons, rescue missions, high crime neighborhoods, prostitution centers, and other places where Satan concentrates his influence. Encourage them and keep them safe. Give me pity for the wretched in my neighborhood. Help me to witness to them.

When you are in the company of wicked people, do they know you are different? 🍵

> "By wisdom a house is built,
> and through understanding
> it is established; through
> knowledge its rooms
> are filled with rare
> and beautiful treasures."
>
> (Prov. 24:3–4)

I used to live in a city that had an annual "Tree Bank Day." People were free to put their old TVs, washing machines, broken chairs, everything too big for the weekly trash collection, out on their tree banks. One day was allowed for others to come by and take whatever they wanted. Then the city truck collected the rest for the dump.

Amazing things turned up. One woman found three pieces of wicker furniture in different places, painted them white, and made a matched set. A friend found a perfectly good crib. Another friend caned two maple chairs without seats, had them refinished and they were beautiful. It is indeed true that one woman's junk is another woman's treasure.

In Solomon's time there were no tree-bank days. The rare and beautiful treasures mentioned here were gold, jewels, perfumes and spices, animal pelts, ivory, and carved wood. When the Queen of Sheba visited Solomon's palace she was overwhelmed, and she was quite opulent herself.

Building a household—a family—takes much wisdom, understanding, and knowledge. There are days when it seems like all we are getting for our effort is junk. Nothing makes the baby stop crying. The children fight. The teacher sends home a letter of complaint. What possible good can come out of this desperate situation? At this point God's call to full-time motherhood has all the appeal of moldy left-overs.

This proverb reminds us that a family is *built*, not created by a magical waving of the hand, and not popped out of a box with easy-to-follow directions for assembly. It is built, day by day, week by week. The labor we expend does matter. We are not decorating our home with cast-off objects, but with rare and beautiful children.

That's God's promise. We can trust Him to honor our efforts, even on the hardest days. Look at the baby, asleep at last. Isn't he a treasure?

Lord, I need your perspective. Sometimes I wonder if I'm worth anything at all. When I don't know what to do, give me wisdom from your Word. When I'm depressed, cheer me with Your presence. I'm important to you, Lord. Thank you.

This week, spend two hours doing something especially nice for yourself. ☕

"Do not gloat
when your enemy falls;
when he stumbles,
do not let
your heart rejoice."

(Prov. 24:17)

God has always had a peculiar concern for our personal enemies. His eye-for-an-eye, tooth-for-a-tooth philosophy was a merciful improvement over the pagan approach to bodily harm. The general practice of the time was: if someone took his enemy's eye, he was bludgeoned to death. God set definite restraints upon punishment. The twenty-first chapter of Exodus details specific penalties for injury due to anger as well as injury due to personal irresponsibility.

God also calls His people to a merciful attitude toward their enemies. This is an even more radical teaching. There is nothing in our human nature which causes us to feel sorry when our enemy stumbles. We really want to say, "You got what's coming to you!"

So the Holy Spirit brings us to that point in our spiritual lives when we can restrain our feelings and our actions. Then Jesus stretches us even further. He says, "Love your enemies and pray for those who persecute you" (Matt. 5:44). Look here, Lord. I won't kill my enemy. I won't gloat when she falls. But I sure don't intend to love her. As for praying—I've got all I can manage just praying for my friends.

Jesus answers, "The pagans love their friends. If you do that, you're not different from them. People will know you are sons of my father when they see you loving your enemies."

That's really being different. How can we do it? Not in our own strength. That kind of love only comes when we belong to Jesus Christ, and have the power of His Holy Spirit. The Holy Spirit comes to live in us and remind us of everything that Jesus said. He gives us power to love our enemies, even as Jesus loved those who persecuted Him.

You will have to help me love my enemies, Lord. I certainly don't feel like doing it. Give me the power of your Spirit to obey your teaching. Take away the gloating and rejoicing that I have when my enemy suffers. Thank you for the peace that comes when hating stops.

Who are your enemies? List them, and pray for one each day. 🍵

"An honest answer is like a kiss on the lips."

(Prov. 24:26)

Anybody who tells me to be honest and say what I really think puts me on guard. People who say they want the truth seldom do, especially if my "truth" does not agree with theirs.

We must be careful then, how we give an honest answer. Note that it should be like a kiss on the lips—loving and tender. We kiss people we know very well. We have earned the right to be intimate. So it is with an honest answer. There has to be a deep relationship before it can be graciously received.

There is an old saying that the truth hurts. In the sense that the realization of truth shows a person she has been wrong and needs to change her behavior, this is so. But even this kind of painful truth can be given and received with love. Yet there is another kind of truth which hurts —the cutting remark delivered by the knife-like tongue. What the speaker says is certainly true, but it is spoken out of resentment, pride, or retaliation. It is thus ineffective to bring change.

The popular expression for this is "cutting someone down." The truthful remark is usually given publicly, causing its receiver to experience humiliation. If it can be humorous to everyone else, so much the better (or worse!). TV situation comedy families are masters at this kind of ego-smashing, with ripostes flying back and forth, each wittier than the last. In real families, the laugh track is missing. The person being cut down suffers intense feelings of worthlessness.

Scripture always equates truth with love. In Ephesians 4, Paul talks about the unity of the body of Christ. As we who are its members help each other, we are to do so lovingly, in such a way that we are joined tightly together, like supporting ligaments. You don't have to be a surgeon to know what a cutting remark can do to a ligament.

Father, I have stabbed many more people than I have kissed. Forgive me. May I earn the right to be honest. May I be honest in a loving way.

Family members can fall into the practice of cutting each other down, and not realize it. What about yours? ☕

165

"Finish your outdoor work and get your field ready; after that, build your house."

(Prov. 24:27)

When Phil and Janet decided to get married, Phil didn't bother with the old-fashioned practice of asking Janet's father for permission. They just sailed into the living room Monday night and stood in front of the TV set to announce their engagement. Janet's father knew that under the circumstances he wasn't going to see the end of the football game, so he turned off the set. "When's the date?" he asked.

They hadn't settled on one yet. They just knew they wanted to get married. "Where are you going to live?" Get an apartment somewhere. "How will you pay the rent?" Well, since Phil was working only part-time at the supermarket and going to community college, Janet would have to drop out of school and get a full-time job. Janet's mother interjected at this point and said she hoped they could find an apartment near a bus line, since Janet didn't have her own car.

Janet's sister, who was eleven, said she thought it would be so neat to have her own apartment filled with new furniture. "We won't have any new furniture," Janet explained hastily. "We'll have to go to garage sales and read the classified ads." Of course, there was that old sofa in the basement. "That old three-legged sofa," her father reminded her.

Janet's mother was sorry to see Janet drop out of school. Couldn't they wait a year? "Don't worry, Mom. I'll go back and finish as soon as Phil is out." What if a baby should come along? "We'll take precautions." Janet's mother thought about her own precautions and how Janet's middle name should have been "Surprise."

Did Phil have any idea how much it would cost to be married—insurance, hospitalization, telephone, etc.? Well, no, he hadn't figured that out yet. Did Janet have any particular full-time job in mind? Oh, there was sure to be *something*. Since she had lived at home all her life, was she really prepared to manage an apartment? "Oh, Daddy, it can't be all that hard." (Janet's mother glanced at the ceiling.)

Janet's father spoke right up and said he didn't think Phil and Janet were prepared to get married. Janet disagreed. Why, Phil already owned two sets of dishes he'd gotten free at the supermarket, and she could come home every Saturday to do the laundry.

Dear God, I think of my own children who will probably be married someday. May their lives be well-ordered before they build their families. May I teach them from your Word and my experience.

"Unless the Lord builds the house, its builders labor in vain" (Ps. 127:1).

"Do not testify against your
neighbor without cause,
or use your lips to deceive.
Do not say, 'I'll do to him
what he has done to me;
I'll pay that man back
for what he did.'"

(Prov. 24:28)

Problems with a neighbor seldom evolve into a court case. Usually the irritation remains, along with the dog that barks incessantly, and the apple tree that drops its wormy fruit on both sides of the fence. The trend toward condominiums puts a neighbor not twenty feet of grass away, but only the width of a wall. Late-night parties, TV programs, fights—all become community property.

The human thing to do is retaliate. If she won't turn down her stereo, I won't either. If she lets trash lie all over the back yard, I won't bother to clean up mine either. If they don't want to be friendly, we don't want to be either. Apartment dwellers stand in the elevator without speaking. The couple in the house two doors away gets a divorce, and no one knows.

Jesus' command that we love our neighbor, coupled with the parable of the Good Samaritan, teaches us that our neighbor isn't necessarily the person living next door. The trouble is, we've moved the neighbor so far away that we forget that she is also the person next door on both sides. That makes it a much harder commandment to keep. I can help a woman in a car accident out on Route 44 much more easily than I can love my grumpy next-door neighbor whose kids run across my lawn.

How can we love someone we don't like? We must ask God for love, to begin with. We must then respond to our neighbor in an uncommon way by doing something kind. The Christian is not to be the silent sufferer, tolerating a problem. (How easy it is to feel like a martyr!) The Christian is to extend herself—take a positive step toward the relationship. The path to neighbor-love may take many steps. But it is so much better than going to court, even for a just cause.

For my good neighbors, I thank you Lord. They have helped me, and I am grateful. For my bad neighbors, I ask you to give me your love for them. Show me what I can do to make their lives happier.

Today take a few minutes to visit with a neighbor you don't like, for Jesus' sake. ☕

"A little sleep,
a little slumber,
a little folding of
the hands to rest—
and poverty will come
on you like a bandit
and scarcity like
an armed man."

(Prov. 24:33)

Just one more hour of television and I'll go to the store." "Just one more hour in bed and I'll get dressed and look for a job." "I'm a low-drive person by nature. Or maybe it's my thyroid."

Here's the sluggard again, finding excuses not to work.

She has good intentions, but they get confused with actually doing something. She thinks talking about cleaning the kitchen floor is as good as getting out the sponge-mop and bucket. If I don't get around to vacuuming our bedroom, I leave the vacuum cleaner out. It makes me feel virtuous.

We must work if we wish to prosper. What about our souls? How do they prosper? By the hard work of daily prayer, the faithful study of the Scriptures, and the assembling together of God's people. These experiences make our souls rich and well-fed with spiritual meat.

But the sluggard's soul? Alas, it is a poverty case. "Just one more hour of tennis and I'll read the Bible." "Just one more load of wash and I'll sit down and pray." "I'm not a church person by nature. Or maybe it's my background."

How easily Satan deceives us. He makes us believe that thinking about spiritual exercise is as good as doing it. If I don't get around to my devotions, I leave my Bible on my desk and feel Spiritual.

Satan is adaptable. He can roar like a lion or talk like a serpent. Sometimes, all he has to do is whisper, "Tomorrow".

Sometimes I get tired, Lord. But I know that sometimes I'm just lazy. Motivate and strengthen me through your Word.

Is there some task you've put off doing? Ask a friend to remind you until you can say, "It's done!" 🍵

"Remove the dross from the silver, and out comes material for the silversmith."

(Prov. 25:4)

This is a political commandment. It concerns those who advise the king. The dross, the refuse metals that rise to the top of the melted ore, must be removed so that the purity and beauty of the silver isn't marred. Likewise, those in authority must purify their staffs, getting rid of any who would corrupt their office.

Those of us in the common citizenry have little to say about who advises the president of the United States, or the governor of our state. But as electors we can directly affect who our leaders will be. We cast a vote, for one thing, but our influence extends far beyond that. We can be informed citizens who discuss the issues with others. We can write letters to our representatives and work in political campaigns. We can also give financial support to those organizations which lobby for Christian principles in government.

In Romans 13, Paul gives specific instructions to citizens. Everyone must submit himself to the governing authorities, for these have been established by God. We are to pay taxes and show respect. In 1 Timothy 2 we are told to pray "for kings and all those in authority, that we may live peaceful, quiet lives in all godliness and holiness." Our peaceful, quiet lives depend upon the godliness and holiness of our leaders as well as ourselves.

It has been estimated that forty percent of Americans are Christians; i.e. they recognize Christ as their Lord and Savior. If a block of voters this large was exercising its responsibility as citizens, would we not see more government leaders who conducted their lives and the affairs of this country on biblical principles? When we choose our silver carefully, we will have much less dross.

Thank you for my country, Lord. I know I take it for granted sometimes. Guide our leaders. Burden them to search your Word for wisdom. Lead them to choose advisors who will tell them the truth, who will be honest, and who will respect authority. By your Spirit, empower me to be a responsible citizen who upholds the Scriptures.

"The punishment which the wise suffer who refuse to take part in the government, is, to live under the government of worse men" (Plato).

"A word aptly spoken is like apples of gold in settings of silver."

(Prov. 25:11)

The question is not whether or not we should speak the truth, but how to do it. To speak the truth in such a way that it is accepted as something which adds beauty to life, is a great gift.

In Ecclesiastes 12:9, we read about a wise teacher who

imparted knowledge to the people: "He pondered and searched out and set in order many proverbs ... (he) searched to find just the right words, and what he wrote was upright and true." To speak the truth is hard work. First, we must be sure it is the truth. How many times have we been absolutely sure of something, only to discover we were mistaken? The source must be reliable, as must be the transmitter. The person who brings a message must be sure that she has heard it correctly, not forgotten any of it, nor colored it with her own feelings.

Imparting the truth is not easy. The sensitivity of the listener also has to be considered. There is a right moment to speak—not at the end of an exhausting day. Sometimes it would be better to listen. The speaker must ask herself if this truth will be an encouragement, a positive force for growth.

Ephesians 4:15 tells us to speak the truth in love. Our attitudes toward our listeners affect how our words will be received. The tone of voice and the look in a person's eyes can convey concern. Yet the truth, even from Scripture, can hurt and can subsequently be rejected, if spoken from an unloving heart. The simile of truth as a two-edged sword is intended for use on our enemies, not our friends.

The apples of gold in settings of silver are thought to be golden balls arranged in silver filigree baskets. These were set on the table as ornaments, much like we use centerpieces today. No doubt they were carefully hand-crafted, valuable, and very beautiful. So should our words be.

Oh God, I know that my words are sometimes like hot peppers instead of apples. Forgive me. Fill me with love so that I may encourage others and make their lives more beautiful.

More about words: Isaiah 50:4. ☕

"If you find honey,
eat just enough
—too much of it,
and you will vomit."

(Prov. 25:16)

Honey is delicious, but a little is satisfying enough. How much of anything pleasant is enough? What is enough fried chicken, lying in the sun, reading a novel, talking with a friend, lobbing a tennis ball? When do we stop working or going to school? Can there ever be too much religious activity? The woman who said she was "sick of Bible studies" may have come closer to this proverb than we think.

First Timothy 4:4, 5 tells us that, "For everything God created is good, and nothing is to be rejected if it is received with thanksgiving, because it is consecrated by the word of God and prayer." If we eat too much pizza, it isn't the pizza's fault.

The third chapter of Ecclesiastes teaches us that there is a "time for everything." To set our priorities in order we need to keep in constant touch with God's Word. This book of perfect balance will enable us to balance our own activities. Further counsel comes from listening to the Word as it is preached by our minister. He has a good vantage point to see where the members of the body of Christ are needing help. Then there are those close Christian friends who know us so well that they can be trusted to speak honestly about our life pattern.

David, in Psalm 25:4 says, "Show me your ways, O Lord, teach me your paths; guide me in your truth." We can learn to eat just enough honey. Delicious as it is, nobody wants to get sick from it.

I just love to eat honey, Lord. I love to do so many things. Thank you for giving me so much to enjoy. Teach me how much is enough. May my priorities be yours.

Take a piece of paper and jot down your main activities for the day, and the time you spend on each. Evaluate yourself. Ask someone in your family, or a Christian friend, to comment also. ☕

> "Better to live
> on a corner of the roof
> than share a house
> with a quarrelsome wife."
>
> (Prov. 25:24)

Dave and Mona had been our next-door neighbors for six years before they moved to Topeka. Every holiday we'd get a greeting card with a note at the bottom, "Come see us!" On Easter we got a phone call, begging us to come out for Memorial Day. We didn't have any other plans, so we said yes. It wasn't that we didn't like Dave and Mona. They were really kind people, never too busy to lend a hand. When I had the flu, Mona fed the family for three days. And Dave helped us put in the patio where we all got together for cook-outs.

But Mona got on our nerves sometimes. She was always picking on Dave, either nagging him to get some chore done, or complaining because he made a mess, like wearing his garden shoes in the house. Mona was one of those super-clean women who equated newspapers scattered around the family room with staph infection.

We arrived in Topeka about eight in the evening, and by the time we got the kids settled down it was after ten. It wasn't until the next morning that we had a chance to take the grand tour of the new house. It was much bigger than the one in our neighborhood, with more room out back for Dave's prized vegetable garden.

After we thought we had seen everything, Mona went into the kitchen to make iced tea. Dave motioned for us to follow him down into the basement again. There, behind a door that we assumed led to a closet, was an eight-by-eight cubicle that was Dave's private hideaway. "Mona doesn't like me to show this to anyone," he explained, "but I wanted you to see it. What do you think?" We looked at the beat-up reclining chair and the floor lamp with its cracked shade. There were books piled on the floor, garden magazines strewn all over the place, and a hot pot and coffee cup that hadn't seen soap for weeks. "I'll have to leave the door open," Dave said, "or we won't hear Mona call when the tea is ready. When the door's closed, this place is practically sound proof."

We stood there and sensed the peace in the midst of the disarray. Just then Mona's voice pierced the stillness. "Tea's ready! Hurry up, Dave, before the ice melts! Try to be on time for once!" My husband put his hand on Dave's shoulder. "It's a great little room, Dave. Just the place for planning a garden." The three of us walked back upstairs before Mona could call us again.

Am I so quarrelsome that my husband needs a corner of the roof? Tell me the truth, Lord.

Even in the best relationships, people do need a private place for meditation. Does everyone in your family have one? ☕

179

"Like one who seizes
a dog by the ears
is a passer-by who
meddles in a quarrel
not his own."

(Prov. 26:17)

When Lyndon Johnson was president of the United States, he got much publicity for holding a hound dog up by its ears. Dog lovers protested, saying he was hurting the dog, but the president claimed the dog didn't mind at all. But at the time this proverb was written, dogs were not household pets. Grabbing an untrained dog by its ears was sure to arouse its anger and result in a sharp bite on the arm.

In the same way, meddlers are asking for trouble. Their interference offends both parties in a quarrel and settles nothing. But didn't Jesus say, "Blessed are the peacemakers"? He certainly did. He settled disputes among his own followers. But he stayed away from strife that didn't belong to him. When asked to decide the division of an inheritance he refused (Luke 12:13, 14).

Scripture does not take meddling lightly. Peter groups it with murdering, stealing, and other criminal acts (1 Pet. 4:15). Surely, busybodies have caused far more trouble in the church than thieves and murderers. There is a certain pleasure in being involved in other people's business. Paul was aware of this and consistently directed those in the church to seek arbitration through their leaders.

Yet, we are not to be indifferent to quarrels. How can we respond? By committing the dispute to God and seeking His will in prayer. There may be opportunity for us to say a helpful word when the anger has cooled down. Our suggestions will then be wiser and more easily received. Or we may be directed through our prayers to continue praying and leave the solution for someone else.

Lord, help me to mind your business and my own business and stop at that.

Deeper reading on quarrels: Galatians 5. ☕

"As iron sharpens iron, so one man sharpens another."

(Prov. 27:17)

Ellie was delighted with her new business partner. She felt that the reason they got along so well was the fact that they had totally different personalities. Ellie was creative, but running off in all directions. Roberta had a strong sense of organization and priorities. Together they built their catering business into a company that grossed $50,000 a year.

There is an old maxim that says if two people are exactly alike, one of them is unnecessary. I thought of this when Dave called me last week to get my opinion on whether he should run for re-election on a corporation board of which I am also a member. "I seem to have different ideas from everyone else," he said. "Great!", I answered. "Our board needs different ideas."

Opposites may attract in dating, but they aren't nearly so attractive in organizations. They are too threatening. The presence of opposites means giving, and maybe losing a little of ourselves, too. Yet out of diversity comes growth. Paul was a great man, but he needed Silas, Barnabas, Titus, Priscilla, and Aquila. The whole sixteenth chapter of Romans is devoted to an appreciation of his friends.

One of the most exciting ways to watch the Holy Spirit at work is to sit in a group of Christians with totally different ideas about how to do something, and see them eventually come to one mind. Proposals pepper the air. Some are rejected. Others are received enthusiastically. Others are modifications as points of view change. One thought sparks another. And out of it all comes a fantastic summer program, an innovative women's organization, or a beautiful new sanctuary.

We begin with like substances—believers in Christ. We interact directly with each other. And we become individually and corporately more effective.

God, I am not very sharp all by myself. I need other people who are different from me. Ease my anxiety when I am in groups. Open my mind to change.

Are you in the midst of organizing a committee? Deliberately choose someone with whom you are not perfectly comfortable. Ask God to bless this relationship. ☕

"If anyone turns
a deaf ear to the law,
even his prayers
are detestable."

(Prov. 28:9)

During sharing time at evening service, a young man got up. He was taking a trip on Monday, and he hadn't found time to get his car inspected nor his license plate renewed. Since he was driving with expired plates, he wanted prayer that he wouldn't be picked up by the police. There was an embarrassing silence in the congregation while the minister tactfully reworded the request.

This proverb is concerned with more than an occasional lapse in our Christian conduct. The reference here is to a habitual and obstinate rejection of God. In this category fall those people who have nothing to do with

God until a crisis, and then they beseech Him for help. Should God in His mercy grant deliverance, they quickly go their own way again.

A deaf ear to the law can also be much more subtle. There is an outward form of godliness—a practicing all the rituals of religion—which conceals an unsaved soul. Sometimes the one who prays the most eloquent prayers is the greatest hypocrite. "These people come near to me with their mouth and honor me with their lips, but their hearts are far from me," says Isaiah 29:13. Jesus used this quotation when talking to the Pharisees and teachers of the law. The church still has to deal with that problem today.

Another form of self-deceit is the person who uses prayer as an excuse to avoid church. She may "commune with nature" on Sunday morning. Or she may say she is going to spend an hour in prayer only to fall asleep after the first petition, or catch her hand on the TV control panel, thus turning it on during her favorite program.

Such ruses do not fool God. He bluntly calls those prayers detestable. But the honest prayer always finds acceptance. The psalmist in Psalm 66 experienced this: "If I had cherished sin in my heart, the Lord would not have listened; but God has surely listened and heard my voice in prayer. Praise be to God, who has not rejected my prayer, or withheld his love from me!" (vv. 18–20).

Father, I rejoice that you forgive my sin and hear my prayers. Thank you for loving me. Thank you for listening to me.

Many things good in themselves can keep us from hearing the law. An informal meeting on the new missions program makes us late for Sunday School class. Caring for the baby is reason to stay home from church. How many others can you name? ☕

"Whoever flatters
his neighbor
is spreading a net
for his feet."

(Prov. 29:5)

As Christian and Hopeful were nearing the Celestial City, they met some shepherds who offered them hospitality. The shepherds, whose names were Knowledge, Experience, Watchful, and Sincere, then pointed them on their way, warning them of temptations that could impede their Pilgrim's Progress. "Beware of the flatterer!" was one piece of advice. Alas, the travelers forgot, and were soon caught in a great net from which they could not escape. At last a Shining One came and cut the net apart, but before the pilgrims could go on, they were soundly whipped to teach them the good way they should walk.

Why does God's Word consider flattery such a great

evil? "May the Lord cut off all flattering lips . . ." says David in Psalm 12:3. Flattery is lying, for one thing. It springs from an insincere heart, and it is intended to puff up the flatterer more than the one flattered. The purpose is to get something in return for the false compliment.

The net is pride, which makes the hearer believe the flatterer. This draws him away from his utter dependence upon God, diminishing His glory. Only the realization of God's displeasure followed by repentance, can restore proper relationship with Him.

All of us need to be encouraged and encouraging. This kind of honest appreciation among believers is so essential that Paul elevates it to the status of a specific gift (Rom. 12:8). This is not flattery—words spoken for our own advantage.

In one of my appearances before a group of church women I gave what I considered to be a hard-driving speech. After the meeting, one woman came up to me, took my hand, and thanked me for my "adorable speech." I knew that was flattery. Other examples are not so obvious and therefore are much more dangerous. Satan himself is the supreme flatterer, masquerading as a servant of righteousness. We are told in 2 Corinthians 11 that he has servants. May none of us fall into that category!

Yes, God, I like to have people say nice things about me. Flattery makes me feel important. Forgive me. But I need encouragement, God. I get awfully low sometimes. Give me discernment that I may know which compliments are sincere and to your glory. And make my words sincere that I may not spread a net for others.

Flattery is a popular device among people wanting to get married. If you fall into this category, ask God for special help. ☕

"The rod of correction
imparts wisdom,
but a child left to itself
disgraces his mother."

(Prov. 29:15)

Notice what kind of rod it is—one of correction. There is no indiscriminate beating implied here, no whack on the bottom out of sheer anger or frustration. This rod is constructive, imparting wisdom.

In Proverbs, wisdom is always related to the law of God. Direction and correction would be a good summary of the teachings intended for parents. Direction is first: "A rebuke impresses a man of discernment more than a hundred lashes a fool" (Prov. 17:10). The law of God is to be taught consistently and modeled by the parents. Eli failed as a teacher; David failed as a model. Both suffered deeply from the rebellion of their sons.

Why is the mother the one highlighted for disgrace? Perhaps because she is the child's early teacher, the one with him day after day in his pre-school years. The time she spends teaching the Word of God during the first five years of the child's life makes an indelible mark.

Another reason may be the possibility that she is more tender-hearted, more easily influenced by the child's winsomeness. She can be persuaded to forego punishment. Fathers are supposedly less readily swayed.

In these days when mothers and fathers often share the raising of small children, the distinction between the sexes may be blurred. In this case, both parents are responsible and both suffer disgrace when the child grows up indifferent to the law.

A child left to herself will surely be a disgrace to somebody. Without direction and correction, the child's behavior will reflect her natural desire to sin. Her heart is stubborn and wants to follow its own desires (Ps. 81:12). It is deceitful above all things and beyond cure (Jer. 17:9). Out of it come evil thoughts, murders, adultery, sexual immorality, theft, false testimony, and slander (Matt. 15:19). Is it any wonder that this stubborn heart must be disciplined by loving parents?

Sometimes I'm too hard on the children, Lord. Sometimes I'm too easy. Help me to discipline them fairly and helpfully. Guide me as I teach them your Word. Open their hearts to its truth.

Busy schedules and television make it difficult for a family to share the Bible together. Talk about this problem with your husband. Begin a set time for Bible teaching. Pray for consistency in spite of diversions. 🍵